THE ULTIMATE COM

# THE ULTIMATE COMMUNION OF MANKIND

A Celebration of Rudolf Steiner's Book
*The Philosophy of Freedom*

Karen Swassjan

TEMPLE LODGE
London

Translated by J. Collis

Temple Lodge Publishing
51 Queen Caroline Street
London W6 9QL

Published by Temple Lodge 1996

Originally published in German under the title *Das Abendmahl des Menschen, Zum hundertsten Geburtstag der 'Philosophie der Freiheit'* by Verlag am Goetheanum, Dornach, Switzerland, 1993

© Verlag am Goetheanum 1993
This translation © Temple Lodge Publishing 1996

The moral right of the author has been asserted under the Copyright, Designs and Patents Act, 1988

All rights reserved. No part of this publication may be reproduced, stored in a retrieval system, or transmitted, in any form or by any means, electronic, mechanical, photocopying, recording or otherwise, without the prior permission of the publishers

A catalogue record for this book is available from the British Library

ISBN 0 904693 82 1

Cover art by Rebecca Thomson, layout by S. Gulbekian
Typeset by DP Photosetting, Aylesbury, Bucks
Printed and bound in Great Britain by Cromwell Press Limited, Broughton Gifford, Wiltshire

# Contents

Translator's acknowledgements
page vii

From the author
page 1

1. The only book worth saving
page 6

2. Abstention from all logic by the conscious mind
page 24

3. Thinking: the eye of the needle
page 36

4. 'The thunderous jubilant cry of the Seraphim'
page 68

5. 'The most Christian of philosophies'
page 86

An essential addition to all New Editions
page 99

# Translator's acknowledgements

Not having been favoured with the freedom the author possessed to re-write his own text when translating it from Russian into German (see 'From the author'), I have drawn heavily on the expertise of others in trying to render it into English. With much gratitude I therefore acknowledge the help given me by Heidi Herrmann-Davey, Anna Meuss and Andrew Welburn.

The English version of many, though not all, of the quotations from Nietzsche is owed to R. J. Hollingdale's translations of *Ecce Homo*, *Thus Spoke Zarathustra*, and *The Anti-Christ*, in the Penguin Books, London (1979, 1969, 1968 editions).

Dear Professor,

In the final analysis I would greatly prefer to be a professor in Basle than God. However, I could not presume to indulge my own private egoism to the extent of neglecting the creation of the world on that account.

*From Nietzsche's last letter to Jacob Burckhardt, dated 6 January 1889.*

# From the author

This book—originally not a book at all but merely the introduction to the first ever edition of *The Philosophy of Freedom* to be published in Russian—was written in Armenia in January this year. The only alternative to embarking on a Darwinistic struggle for survival (in the 'mausoleum'-length bread queues as well as in an unlit apartment where the water stored in the bath might just as well have been drawn up through a hole in the ice) was to knuckle down and get on with the business of writing an introduction to *The Philosophy of Freedom*. The rule of the day was Nietzsche's: What does not kill me makes me stronger; and, sure enough, the entropic winter did indeed fail to finish me off. Some lovers of bombast might be inclined to add: 'No wonder. Isn't that always the case when we turn to the spirit!' Perhaps they're right, but not being much given to bombast myself I remain astonished that life can go on when according to all the rules of breeding and good taste it would have been more fitting to take leave of it in justifiable, though perhaps bombastic, silence. Let those who so much enjoy waffling on about the power of the spirit test it not in their courses of speech formation but *on site* in places where at least eleven of the ten commandments are daily and nightly broken.

It then transpired that introductions, too, follow their own destiny. I decided to fall in with the kind suggestion of the publisher and make this introduction written in *Russian* into a *German* book. Naturally, the question of translation then came up—a more than risky undertaking, I always feel. Since the ancient Orphics and Plato declared the word, once spoken, to be no more than a coffin for the thought, *what* exactly do we translate when we translate? My scepticism conjured up the image of translation as a second burial (not without desecration of the corpse), a picture that may be unjust in specific cases but holds good in the general rule. The only solution that would, it seemed to me, result in merely minimal losses was, therefore, to take on the translation myself, without forgetting that so-called translation would in this instance turn out to be one long sin against the rules of translating. Not that I intended a complete re-write. On the contrary, I made every effort to put the existing Russian text into German as accurately as I could, but I treated the whole thing as a new original work. In short, I masqueraded as the author when I should have been acting merely as my own translator.

It goes without saying that the theme of the book obliged me to maintain an appropriate attitude, which meant that the whole undertaking turned out to be a good opportunity to give yet another practical proof of the principles represented in it. I didn't allow the otherwise meticulous reproduction of the original text to deteriorate into pedantry, so if an obstinate passage raised its hackles at the prospect of being transplanted, behaving like a right-wing radical, I left it where it wanted to stay, in its untranslatable 'blood and soil', and respectfully appealed instead directly to the genius of the German language. The end result (noticeable only after the event) is a remarkable linguistic hybrid: a Russian original with a good many passages impossible to render in German, and the German re-write, full of passages that cannot be put into Russian. Be that as it may, this harmless double trap means that no future grumbler comparing the two versions will have the right to catch me *in flagrante delicto*, crying: 'That's wrong,' or, 'This isn't right.' Should it arise, I shall retort as in E. T. A. Hoffmann's delightful fantasy: Accused of improvising embellishments on a piece by Gluck, the unknown minstrel calmly withdraws to another room, only to reappear some moments later in powdered wig and with hand on hilt, declaring: 'But I *am* Sir Gluck!'

Without a doubt I would have expressed everything differently had I written the whole text in German from the first, for wryly we remark when something has reached completion: It turns out to contain not so much what has been said as what has remained unsaid. Only now do I sense, decidedly, what I should actually have written about *The Philosophy of Freedom*. (A self-deceptive manoeuvre, for I know in advance that this decidedness will increase and grow stronger with every new attempt at presenting the subject. Well, then! May it be blessed for that.) To forestall any future (*intelligent!*) criticism I can say: These are beginnings, half-captured creatures, hesitant blendings of colours for future 'paintings', for I shall continue to write and talk about *The Philosophy of Freedom* as long as my life lasts—and a good distance beyond as well. What follows here must be taken as a tuning fork to whose vibrations an orchestra may temper its instruments.

Initially I intended to build into the text a number of ideas that hadn't occurred to me until after the Russian version was finished. I began to realize, for example, that what Rudolf Steiner calls *thinking* may be compared with the concept of *existence* in more recent versions of existentialism, although it makes the latter, puffed up as it is, look rather like a bubble floating up from the cerebral froth of various philosophical idols. You only have to consider where this 'existence' is always to be found in the works of these idols, from Bergson perhaps, to Jaspers and Sartre: in all kinds of mystical (or misty!), conceptual dross such as *élan vital, chiffre de transcendence,* or even Sartre's *la nausée,* but not at all in *thinking* which has been so thoroughly compromised by the positivist opposition party that all they can do is track down the metaphysical validity of life in functional disorders. To crown it all, these bully boys with their diplomas and their attitudes of unassailability have the arrogant gall to draw a veil of silence over *Steiner*! I hope very much that some degree of apocalyptic shake-up will in due course irrupt even among modern philosophers!

Another insight which began to dawn on me was that the whole immense cosmic and earthly deed of Christ was nothing other than the overpowering blaze of a unique *moral imagination* in which the most exalted Sun Being sacrificed himself voluntarily for the earth, knowing that this earth might otherwise have lost its meaning in the way it was evolving.

I further realized that the word 'unique', normally only employed as a stylistic ornament, must be taken entirely literally when applied to *The Philosophy of Freedom*. This book is unique not only within the period of the Kali Yuga, whose *exodus* it has become, but over the whole extent of cosmic and earthly human history *ab initio creaturae*. Characteristic for the evolution of mankind—since the time of Old Saturn—has been the fact that the human being as *an evolving creation* has always been thought out, formed, nurtured, dominated, bred and led from outside (initially by the direct presence of the divine, then gradually by various authoritarian surrogates, i.e. priests, commandments, rules, morals, rights, etc.). The outcome of this process has inevitably meant that the increasing sovereignty of the human being— identical as this is with the increasing internalization of that leadership or tutelage formerly imposed from outside— could not help but culminate in the worship of the ego that has found its most striking expression in the God-denying individualism of modern times. The *uniqueness* of *The Philosophy of Freedom* lies in the fact that FOR THE FIRST TIME it has become possible for the luciferic saying of the Old Testament, '*Ye shall be as gods*' (Gen. 3,5; see also Ps. 82,6), to combine with the Christian '*I said, Ye are gods*' (John 10,34). In other words, the human being, who for aeons has been thought by the gods, now at last begins to think for himself, no longer in the a-cosmic, Cartesian sense of the word where the universal principle 'thinking' becomes the capitalist private property of the head, but cosmically and divinely. Seen radically, this can only mean: Henceforth the only one (yes, as in Max Stirner) responsible for world creation (hitherto uniquely the privilege of divine thinking) is the human being free in thought and free in action. (Don't panic, dear contemporaries! It is not we who are meant, but—let's not indulge in any illusions—RUDOLF STEINER himself who is, so far, the only human being to have succeeded in accomplishing that of which no god would nowadays be capable.)

All these points, and a good many others as well, I might belatedly have incorporated here, but I desisted for the simple reason that they would allow me once again—again for the very first time—to write about *The Philosophy of Freedom*. If James Joyce was right in saying that every writer has only a single novel in his ink-well, then in my case this goes for *The Philosophy of Freedom*. I simply can't conceive of any other subject.

On a more personal note: Augustine said so beautifully, 'I had not yet known love, but already I was in love with love.' Extraordinary though it may seem, I loved *The Philosophy of Freedom* long before I first held the book in my hands and read it. I came across isolated mention of it, indications, quotations, and fell head over heels in love, in love unto death and beyond death, like a juvenile, glowingly, in the manner of Knut Hamsun. Only with Nietzsche had I earlier had a similar experience, but that was after I had *read* him, when I had read his works *to bits*, whereas here it was a matter of an as yet unread book, one I hadn't even seen.

I am happy that destiny has so kindly granted me the privilege of honouring the one hundredth birthday of *The Philosophy of Freedom* here near Dornach in this manner.

Basle, August 1993<br>Karen Svasyan

# 1. The only book worth saving

Not so much from a sense of tact, perhaps, as from a wish for a closer match with what he saw around him, Rudolf Steiner once slightly adapted the Gospel words: '...neither cast ye your pearls before swine...' by switching within the symbolism of the farmyard from those swine of tradition to more ordinary hens. What he said in the second lecture of *The Occult Significance of the Bhagavad Gita*\* strikes home with the full force of a parable: 'If a pearl is lying in the roadway and a hen finds it, the hen does not value the pearl. Most men and women today are hens in this respect. They do not value the pearl that lies there in full view before them. What they value is something quite different. They value their own ideas.'

Though spoken in a different context, these words also apply in every way to our present concern: Of all the pearls lying there in full view before us *The Philosophy of Freedom* surely remains the most unnoticed. Ignoring this inestimable gift from the spirit, the twentieth century, upon whose threshold it was written and whose threshold it has become, has given pride of place instead to the trashily glittering trinkets of its own home-grown ideas, whether they be Marxist, Freudian, existentialist, positivist, neo-positivist, post-neo-positivist or heaven knows what else...

Ernest Renan's excellent rule: 'If one wishes to emphasize the importance of an idea one must first blot it out completely and then demonstrate what the world would become without it,' does not in this instance require the

---

\* R. Steiner, *The Occult Significance of the Bhagavad Gita* (GA 146), tr. G. & M. Adams (New York, Anthroposophic Press, 1968).

subjunctive 'would'. Indeed this might be the opportune moment to celebrate a peculiar anniversary—in the manner of Belshazzar's feast, let it be said—the centenary, namely, of a date since when this book has been systematically ignored, overlooked even, by all manner of cultural mercenaries whose intention was certainly *not* to stress its importance. Yet Renan's rule remains in force—whether it is applied heuristically or merely expresses the 'holy simpletonism' of those hens puffed up with their own ideas. In essence the last hundred years might very well be described as 'the centenary balance sheet of an unread book'; our world, the world in which we live, is the world that has passed by *The Philosophy of Freedom*. They who have eyes, let them see!

Sure enough, I am at once interrupted from the left and from the right, almost in unison, by both 'outsiders' and 'Insiders'. The 'outsiders'—tactfully, indulging our whim, not quite looking us in the eye, and not without a little grain of arrogant irony, expostulate: 'How can you say such a thing! What a fanciful notion to maintain that the fate of the world hangs on a single book whether read or unread!' Thus they speak, winking at one another in self-satisfied fashion. It would be pointless to enter into any discussion: let them peck and scratch away at the glass beads of their own favourite ideas cobbled together from all manner of books—ideas which proclaim that the fate of the world depends on the 'objective course of history' or on 'God's will', or some such *words* from nowhere in particular learned by rote and repeated mechanically. I, however, remain attached to my 'fanciful notion': for surely *those books, whether read or left unread, are the very thing that is sending the world hurtling towards destruction* ... Let anyone show me even a single event in history that can be unmasked without applying the rule *cherchez le livre*? 'Reading is an obsessive occupation,' suggested Seneca in one of his epistles, remembering too late what a fateful part an excessive literary training had played in the moral development of his pupil Nero. We may readily agree with Seneca's exclamation so long as we complement it with its equally correct reverse: 'and so is our failure to take in what we read!'

The 'insiders' get closer to the crux of the matter in their reproachful reply: 'How can you say the book is unread when in fact it is quite definitely regularly read—though perhaps not by many?' I know that it is, of course, but that's not what I mean. There is no better description than Rudolf Steiner's own in the seventh lecture in *From Symptom to Reality in Modern History*\* apropos of the then new edition of *The Philosophy of Freedom*. The passage is specifically about those who *do read* the book:

'People did not judge me on what I gave but in accordance with clichés and stereotypes ... On the whole it hardly mattered what I said myself ... what I myself put into print. People did read it, but reading something isn't necessarily the same as understanding it ... People did not judge what I had actually said or written. Instead some went by what they considered to be mystical, others by what they thought theosophical meant, yet others by all kinds of other criteria ... It was not exactly a pleasure, or even ideal, to publish a new edition of *The Philosophy of Freedom* under such circumstances.' And yet: The matter stood, and still stands here, on the foundation of the *ideal*. While assuming that justice cannot be done to this book by merely *reading* it, we also have to admit that simply *experiencing* it will also hardly do it justice. In the biblical sense I would say that it must be *eaten up*, as in the overwhelming image linking the Book of Ezekiel with the Revelation of John: 'And I went unto the angel, and said unto him, Give me the little book. And he said unto me, Take it and eat it

---

\* R. Steiner, *From Symptom to Reality in Modern History* (GA 185), tr. A.H. Parker (London, Rudolf Steiner Press, 1976).

up; and it shall make thy belly bitter, but it shall be in thy mouth sweet as honey.' (Rev. 10,9)

It would indeed be a horrible mistake to assume this 'little book' to be nothing but a book. Speaking mathematically, the position it holds within the overall literary estate of Rudolf Steiner is that of an infinitely distant point towards which the whole gigantic parabola of his *three-hundred-and-fifty-four-volumed* impetus is directed. Remove it from the scene—a more than absurd idea—and in place of anthroposophy we should be left with that theosophical or brahminical 'doppelgänger' to which it is inseparably bound. The sun-filled gesture of eurythmy is frozen solid when a lifeless emergency brake is applied by all kinds of yogi-magicians; and in place of the *purest* thought that remains true to its testing by Aristotle and Hegel even where countless 'Cassandras' have been busy since time immemorial, we find ourselves faced with a tangle of all kinds of poses and hypnoses deriving from a growling, unhealthy occultism.

Asked which of his books he would most want to see rescued if catastrophe should come upon the world, Rudolf Steiner replied without hesitation: '*The Philosophy of Freedom*'. At first glance this might seem to be an answer arising from subjective preference. He certainly *loved* this book: the *most lonely* of men, the *most lonely* of books. An extremely moving letter is extant, written to Rosa Mayreder in November 1894 following the publication of *The Philosophy of Freedom*. The rolling thunder of this letter, Beethovenesque indeed, leaves us in no doubt as to the state of mind in which the author brought the book into the world:

'I'm not *teaching*; I'm describing what I have inwardly experienced. I'm describing it as I have experienced it. Everything in my book is personal, including the shape of the thoughts. A person who is fond of teaching might expand on the theme. Perhaps a time will come when I myself can do so. But my first wish was to show the biography of a soul struggling up towards freedom. There is nothing you can do in such circumstances to help those who insist on joining you in scaling cliff-faces and crossing abysses. It's as much as you can do to get across yourself. The inner urge to reach the goal burns too strongly to allow for stopping and explaining to others how they might find the *easiest* way over. Also, I believe I would have come to grief had I tried to find suitable paths for others at the same time. I took my own path and followed it as well as *I myself* was capable; and afterwards *this* was the path I described. Later I would be able to find a hundred ways for others to travel. But at the beginning I didn't want to put any of these down on paper. I jumped over boulders in my own, individual manner, I hacked my way through thickets to find the path that suited my own way of working. You don't know what it is to reach the goal until you get there. Perhaps the time for teaching things such as this concern of mine is finished anyway. My interest in philosophy is restricted almost entirely to the experience of the individual...'\*

Condensed into this almost confessional extract is the whole *romantic* energy of the century, from Byron and Schumann right up to Nietzsche. In order to gain an idea of *how The Philosophy of Freedom* was written, we must turn to the chapter in Nietzsche's *Ecce Homo* that describes the state

---

\*R. Steiner, *Briefe*, Vol. II (GA 39) (Rudolf Steiner Verlag: Dornach, 1987, p. 232). Comparing the style of this *personal* letter with that of the book reveals an astonishing contrast between the all-consuming passion of the author speaking about his book and the supreme composure in the tone of the *book* itself. Such was his self-control in the midst of problems that others only managed to deal with by *shouting* about them (Stirner, Nietzsche, Strindberg, Konstantin Leontev, Léon Bloy *inter alios*). Consider the metaphysical snare set by Heidegger using Nietzsche as an example: Thinking does not tolerate shouting, yet there are things that can only be said by shouting. Show me a book other than *The Philosophy of Freedom* that so calmly manages to expose this snare as rubbish!

of mind out of which *Zarathustra* arose—it is crystalline with introspective rapture ('This is *my* experience of inspiration; I do not doubt that one has to go back thousands of years to find anyone who could say to me "It is mine also".'). Yes, indeed, we must be aware of the states of high tension in which *masterpieces are brought to birth*—regardless of whether they are artistic or philosophical, for a masterpiece always bursts the bounds of conventional aesthetics.

Listen once more: '... I believe I would have come to grief had I tried to find suitable paths for others at the same time.' And again: 'Perhaps the time for teaching things such as this concern of mine is altogether finished anyway.' Take note that this is said by one who only a few years on will appear before the world as a *teacher*, or let us say as a TEACHER in the hope that the visual impact of upper-case lettering may somehow force us to take this in. Contradictory, or even nonsensical? Please yourself. Each one of us must find an individual answer in such things, and each will do so in accordance with the measure of freedom he or she has *eaten* and *digested*. That the *teacher of freedom* could not appear wearing the traditional, stereotyped mask of a 'master' with gawping disciples hanging on his every word; that the *teacher of freedom*, above all else, had to be *free* himself, free, even, of the ceremonial claptrap of *teaching*, which meant not the tiniest word of teaching could pass his lips before he had received a powerful *inoculation against teachings*—of this there can be no doubt.

Later, of course, he was to outline numerous sketches of the *general* path. The book *Knowledge of the Higher Worlds*\* becomes a 'philosophy of freedom' *for every man and woman*. But for this to be achieved there were and always will be two merciless conditions. First of all he had to test on

---

\*R. Steiner, *Knowledge of the Higher Worlds—How is it Achieved?* (GA 10), tr. D. Osmond & C. Davy (London, Rudolf Steiner Press, 1985).

himself (as described in the letter quoted) the vaccine of freedom—a most dangerous discovery (called 'nihiline' by Nietzsche) that is capable of turning either into a *shining morality* or else pure 'Sodom'. And secondly, *The Philosophy of Freedom* will only cease to be 'the experience of the individual' and become an experience for 'all', when these 'all' cease to be asylum seekers at any kind of public 'soup kitchen' whatsoever, including the anthroposophical one. That is, when they become *their own master*, namely neither 'steinerites' carrying on their backs a whole sack full of someone else's wisest sayings to suit all situations in life and death (do the opponents of anthroposophy, who judge the latter according to the impression these people make, realize what Rudolf Steiner's own opinion of such 'steinerites' was and how much they made him suffer?), nor any other '... ites,' but each for himself an *ego*, of all things.\*  Nietzsche's 'seven pelts of solitude', reeking so cheekily of social outcasts, are a must, to be tried for size by any soul aspiring to the morning coat of social respectability (in order that this morning coat may be a perfect fit and not droop like a sack).

A romantic challenge to solitude this may be, yet in a key so different! Ponder once more the passage cited earlier: 'I hacked my way through thickets to find the path that suited my own way of working.' Coming from a romantic this

---

\* Here just one of a thousand possible examples: 'It would be interesting to find out how many of the people in our movement who are now reading *The Philosophy of Freedom* would have read it on its own merits, without knowing anything about me and our movement, if it had fallen into their hands back in the early 1890s. How many people would have read it back then and how many would have said, "I can't get through this tangled web of thoughts; it just doesn't make any sense."' (*Community Life, Inner Development, Sexuality and the Spiritual Teacher*, GA 253, tr. E. Creeger, New York, Anthroposophic Press, 1991, lecture of 14 September 1915). Could there be an opponent of anthroposophy who might hit on the idea of proposing a test like this?

would have sounded like a *lamentation*, for a romantic bragging about his solitude would have seized every opportunity to bewail it. Here, by contrast, it sounds almost like a *justification*: Yes, I went my own way and could do nothing to help others; the inner urge to reach the goal burned too fiercely for that to be possible; some time in the future, perhaps, I shall be able to assist others. The *pathos of aloofness* and *militant individualism* are presented here quite clearly from the perspective of a future when they will be overcome. In terms of music it is not the sombre, humiliating minor key hypnotically dragging the soul down into the abyss of inexpressible 'Tristanisms' but a bright and elevating *major* key robustly healing it. Paul Valéry put it beautifully in his character portrait of Leonardo da Vinci: 'No yawning abyss appeared before his eyes, for an abyss made him dream of a bridge.'*

The theme of the Unground (in Boehme's sense) of *The Philosophy of Freedom* would be a more than dangerous one to touch on. Indeed, to speak of 'abysses' at all, when the book is as clear as daylight, can genuinely startle readers who demand to know what 'abysses' might be meant when not a page of it casts any shadow whatsoever.

Thus is the modern individual's comprehension stereotyped: he can discern an abyss only when the *fact* of its presence is sufficiently *advertised* and when it has been talked to shreds with *words*. Or: If you wish to claim acquaintance with the abyss, be so good as to proclaim it abroad at every corner, or at the very least shoot yourself as did Heinrich von Kleist, starve yourself as did Gogol, babble idiotically like Baudelaire or cut off one of your ears as did Van Gogh. Evidently we lack a more educated, noble, indeed adult taste that would enable us to realize right away that one can refrain from doing any of these things and yet be an expert on abysses of a kind that even the most

---

*Paul Valéry, *Oevres*, Part 1, Paris 1957, p.1210.

*fin-de-siècle décadent* has never dreamt of. This is the very kind of abyss that lies in *The Philosophy of Freedom*. They are neither talked about nor do they paralyse, so strongly directed is our glance to the bridges that cross and tame them.*

In the final analysis, then, what was it—apart from the unfathomable nuances of an author's favouritism—that caused the originator of *The Philosophy of Freedom* to claim for this particular book the prerogative of being saved from the conflagration of some future catastrophe? Without hesitation we can reply: Provided the methods of palaeontological reconstruction can be applied to matters of the mind it will be possible to reproduce from this book the outlines of the subsequent works of anthroposophy. I am reminded in this connection of Dostoevsky's shocking formulation: 'If,' he said, 'you could prove mathematically to me that truth lay outside of Christ, then I would prefer to remain with Christ rather than with the truth.' Applying this formulation to our present theme (which is, actually, the same) I say: If you could prove mathematically to me that anthroposophy lay outside *The Philosophy of Freedom*, then in every event I would rather remain with *The Philosophy of Freedom* than with anthroposophy. What, indeed, *is* anthroposophy itself except the total mobilization of knowing inherent in and suitable for *our* time and the spirit of *our* age!

We should take note: Only the occult *Who* can validate the occult *What* and the occult *How*. The *What* of occultism signifies the codex of timeless occult 'truths' learnt by adepts in every age and every place, a kind of transcendental paradigm of occult *syntax* in which any holy saying can be expressed nowadays by a compatriot of Charlie Chaplin or Idi Amin just as much as used to be done by

---

* Those who might find this comparison too metaphorical probably need reminding of the original sense of the ancient Roman *Pontifex* who combined the rank of *priest* with the craft of *bridge-builder*.

those of Shuppiluliuma or, if you will permit me to say so, of Kassiapatatagata. This psychological and mental sloth masquerading as a virtue, losing sight of the importance of such as Hegel while unquestioningly allowing itself to be counted among *those who know*, is in the end merely a kind of rascally 'knowing' uncertified by any true cognition but remaining for ever a refuge for all kinds of obsessed manipulators with murky sensual and supersensual pasts, and for the crowds of inept fanatics who purely by chance kowtow before Krishna, no less, rather than some long-haired and tattooed pavement idol. What an occult villainy this is, and how it makes one hold one's nose at the mere mention of the word 'occultism'! (Who can tell how much damage has been done to *genuine* occult knowledge by this mass psychosis concerning the occult *What*? And how many noble minds who have approached the threshold of the spiritual world by their own efforts have been and still are forced to eschew any contact with the 'occult' in order to retain their respectability!)

Occultism—assuming that so thoroughly discredited a term can be revitalized at all—only begins with the occult *How*. If it is subjected to the (in the Kantian sense) transcendental question: 'How is occult knowledge possible?,' the answer (which Kant was not even capable of conceiving) comes back something like this: It is possible as a radical thinking-through-to-the-end, feeling-through-to-the-end, willing-through-to-the-end of all the forms of knowledge appropriate to a particular era.

The occultism, for example, of the Vedanta proved legitimate (and thus *feasible*) from the seventh pre-Christian century onwards; it was in focus during the period of time when it most accorded with the level of thought and perception of a particular period in *history*. Thereafter it slowly moved away from the focus of history, gradually yet inexorably. Still in the time of Plotinus and right up to Scotus Erigena, infirm though it had become, it retained a purely heuristic significance as a stimulus, an impulse, an incentive, even an amicable ally confirming a newer experience, one that *conformed more with the new level of knowledge meanwhile attained*. However, as it grew ever more infirm and weak this occultism began, from a certain moment (which can, though, not be pin-pointed in a particular year or even a particular century, so elusive are the powers of historical transformation) to function as an obstacle, a brake, indeed as poison.

Useful though it may still have been for a Neo-Platonist, what purpose could it possibly claim to serve in the case of a Cartesian? Descartes as a convert to Buddhism presents a picture of such absurdity that to imagine it one would be advised to look for a Eugene Ionesco among the authors of the book of destiny. What would science and what would Buddhism have gained from it, not to mention the main perpetrator of the muddle himself? It would most decidedly be inadvisable to convert Descartes to Buddhism, although if absolutely necessary a Buddhist might be converted to Cartesianism to enable inner knowledge to save Cartesianism from intellectual sclerosis and Buddhism from becoming a fashionable vogue and a means of weakening the mind.

Rudolf Steiner expressed this in strong enough terms, and he was not speaking purely figuratively: If a pupil of Vyasa, Kapila or Shankara had strayed into our time he would have studied not the Sankhayana or the Vedanta but Fichte, Schelling and Hegel. Only a chain of metamorphoses rhythmically expressing the spirit of each age in turn can ensure the rightness and legitimacy of an occultism. Enduring the discomfort of the lotus position while hoping for the appearance of the millennial mahatmas of Tibet is not merely not on our present agenda; it also means missing out on Tibet itself, which may today more easily be found in Moscow, Geneva or New York than in the Himalayan mountains.

Witness is borne to today's yearning for occult knowledge by dozens of breakthroughs in thought that have occurred despite the fact that thinking has already allowed itself to be nailed down in the coffin of scientific materialism and put on a par with bodily secretions. Clearly it was either supposed to dissolve without more ado into the physiology of cerebral processes, or it was destined to rise again in an entirely new quality. There was no way that it would be able to maintain its present status of an ambiguous 'something' that kept itself going by means of scholastic imitations while at the same time attracting derision of the choicest positivist kind.

A clear alternative therefore appeared and was set in train by Kant. That most malicious Jacobin of thinking achieved in real terms in Königsberg what had only succeeded theatrically in Paris, as though all that pseudo-classical racketing of the French Revolution with the comtesses' heads spiked on to lances, and the buffoonery performed in such bad taste in Notre Dame de Paris, served merely as a spectacle to distract the masses, while that genuine 'Robespierre' in the backwoods got on undisturbed with the only truly necessary buffoonery. Kant beheaded traditional meta-physics and made merely-physics the nurse of thinking. The pseudo-Thermidor then conducted by this most crafty of all regicides ran its course in typically English fashion. *Morality* was kitted out with the highest constitutional rights while the procedures of purely analytical dissection retained for themselves the whole range of *executive power*. The echoes of those events were not heard until decades later, though then not only in the systems of so-called Neo-Kantians but in the whole mood of the century (the last one as well as our own):

If people dissected frogs for six days a week while claiming love, feelings of reverence, or patriotism to be nothing but chemical reactions taking place in the brain, and then on the seventh day went to church with eyes cast-down in innocence (rather like the late Tom Sawyer in front of his Aunt Polly), *this was Kant*. Or if they came to explain human behaviour in accordance with the model of salivating dogs while at the same time reverently believing in God, *this, too, was Kant*. Or, finally, if it became possible to invent all kinds of bombs with the 'intellectual' section of the brain only to bemoan their explosion with the 'moral' section (Oppenheimer is a case in point, but their name is Legion) *this was the same Kant all over again*.

Ever since it came into existence human thinking has fallen many times, but never has it experienced a crash like this one. It reached a complete dead-end. (Those 'thinkers' might at least have maintained an embarrassed silence about this, but no: it had to be extolled with a marked degree of masochism—Du Bois-Reymond's *'ignoramus et ignorabimus'*.) As if this were not enough there also appeared the unavoidable perspective of moral hypocrisy (*cant* has more than a phonetic resemblance to Kant) or, briefly and more as Kant might have put it: the starry sky, with the 'poets' still clucking, above a head in which the 'military-industrial complex' ruled, while the moral laws caused the breast to swell to bursting point in powerless yet upright indignation at the mischief emanating from the head.

It is understandable that thinking, not yet entirely broken, had to counter-attack without delay. This is where we find the powerful creations of German idealism, the mere sight of which sets a millstone turning in the head of anyone stuck in the ways of Kant. Unfortunately that is all they achieved, for being without any kind of epistemological foundation they were soon seized upon by all sorts of subterranean rats. Something else to be found here is the maddening rage of the Romantics pealing a thousand cracked bells above a century gone deaf; and also Schopenhauer's 'Will': while formally obeying the regulations of Kantian customs and excise, it infected the century with lurid symbols from the ancient Upanishads.

Longing for the occult was eating into the whole body of Europe, covered as it was in positivistic sores, while thinking was constantly forced to look for support in hidden places: in Buddhism, in Christian mysticism, in the magical, mythical glow of Neo-Platonism, in efforts to revive ancient ritual gestures. Even the mightiest minds of the age (Baader, Schelling in his later writings) had to turn towards the past in their longing for an *exodus* from this new captivity. All was in vain. The question: 'How is occult knowledge possible?' (by which was meant the *new* occult knowledge *that takes into account the reign of materialism*) hung like a sword of Damocles above all these endeavours, above the purely speculative ones brought to birth in Faustian seclusion and above the pragmatic ones that broke in upon the agenda of everyday life (the founding of the Theosophical Society in 1875). The breed of agnosticism fostered by Du Bois-Reymond was impervious to every kind of Buddhism and every form of Christian mysticism. The 'Achilles heel' of this dragon, the death-blow for this otherwise invincible monster, lies in the call: Let's go, right through it and out the other side, without any longing for ancient Mysteries but with the will to seek the new! Any longing for the old merely elicits a scornful grin and makes the dragon all the stronger. 'Your longing,' he never fails to say, 'merely demonstrates the wretchedness of your knowledge; it interests no one but the psychoanalyst.' Thus he speaks on every occasion; one must be truly and heavily addicted to longing if one fails to hear a ring of *metallic* rightness about these words. Brother meditants: stop all this nonsense! It's ludicrous, anyway, to run with paper swords at this alloy of all metals that negate the cosmos!

The only way out of the impasse was to conquer the situation *from within* and metamorphose the cul-de-sac into the new path of knowledge. We shall see that it was the destiny of *The Philosophy of Freedom* to become the reply to the question about the possibility of finding an occult knowledge in circumstances where the scientific view of nature reigned supreme.

Let us answer the question posed above: Why, to accord with the wish of its author, should we rescue this particular book, or indeed *only* this book, if a catastrophe were to occur? We have given the answer already, so it merely remains to put it succinctly:

Because from this book on its own we could reconstruct the whole mighty organism of Rudolf Steiner's works, emphatically occult as they are, if not literally then in spirit, by following the method used in it. (Steiner once likened the text of *The Philosophy of Freedom* to a musical score that permitted an individual interpretation by every one of us.) Because in the immense labyrinth of cosmic and earthly wisdom this book is the only Ariadne-thread capable of leading the wanderer back to the starting point. And finally, because armed with this book one can plunge regardless even into the least-known depths of occult experience without becoming either a fanatic or a sectarian, a mental patient or merely a figure of fun.

The human race comes of age in our time, and the only necessity besetting us on all sides is the *necessity to become free*, free of anything intent on sticking to our mind like the shirt of Nessus and intent on masquerading as ourselves, be it in the guise of a 'moral' or an 'immoral' mask, a 'divine' truth or a 'devilish' temptation. All these are nothing but yellowing labels suitable for the *old Adam*; for the *new Adam* they are meaningless. In the traditional sense there is no longer any such thing as the moral or the immoral, the divine or the devilish. There is now ONLY the *trial by freedom, clothing-oneself-in-freedom*, on which the fate of all those old labels now hangs.

To lose track of this fact, to assume all those unalterable convictions of yester-year, is tantamount to succumbing to the power of senselessness and paradox, like looking for something not where we have lost it but where the electric light happens to have been switched on (my contemporaries, do you recognize yourselves?). The valiant Baron Münchhausen, not of sound mind, endeavouring to pull himself by his wig out of the mire into which he has fallen, *in consequence of which* he is found worthy of the Nobel prize—what an unsightly image of ourselves this would be as we defiantly refrain from clothing ourselves in freedom and continue to count on some heavenly 'Lordship' or other. But stop! Yesterday's 'lords' will today *without exception* turn into idols wherever we succeed in remaining 'servants'. Or put more plainly: Yesterday the Divine was not in the least dependent on how the 'servants of God' behaved towards it; today the Divine seeks subservience no longer but *solely* collaboration. If we persist in clutching at the comfort of 'being subservient' we shall find ourselves serving not a Divinity but *another master* who is cunningly deploying the empty (yes, yes, I mean the a priori) shell of the Divine. Neither hurrying conscientiously to church ('God's garment laid aside,' as Christian Morgenstern so wonderfully put it) nor learning all 354 volumes of Rudolf Steiner by heart would protect us against this. One wonders whether the author of *The Philosophy of Freedom* wasn't suffocated by us then and whether he isn't *still suffocating now*. We certainly deserve the highest mark ever for passing our test in dissimulation, confusion and bungling: the two-thousand-year history of Christianity, unanimously transformed into anti-Christianity, is arrayed behind us.

Yonder, in solitude and misunderstood, stands *Paul* sounding the only fitting note for the whole two thousand years of Christianity: 'For, brethren, ye have been called unto liberty.' (Gal. 5,13.) (From what mis-tuned instrument, then, did those two millennia get their pitch?) Here, in solitude and misunderstood, stands *Steiner* at the threshold of the third millennium, sounding the same note once again, with unprecedented force. So what now? We must keep calm! There will not be another repetition. We shall either have music emanating from this note, or else—weeping and gnashing of teeth.

Obviously it is beyond our strength to solve this dilemma *globally*. But it is not beyond our strength to solve it *individually*. We have to understand that while a *Philosophy of Freedom* as his own *individual* achievement led Rudolf Steiner to what he called a spiritual science oriented towards anthroposophy, the portal through which he passed to get there *was only large enough to permit the passage of a single individual* at a time. Consequently it would be impermissible, indeed an occult impoliteness, for us all to squeeze our way through in a crowd in the hope that we might slip by undetected. One thing only is written above that portal (those who cultivate occult terminology may substitute 'threshold' for 'portal'): the sentence formulated by the young Rudolf Steiner in his commentary on Goethe's scientific writings: 'TRUTH IS ALWAYS ONLY THE INDIVIDUAL TRUTH OF SIGNIFICANT HUMAN BEINGS.'*

Consider the irrevocable force of those two shocking adverbs: ALWAYS and ONLY. They tell us that no truth can exist if there is no *individual significance* or at least no *will to be significant*. Truths emanating from insignificant members of the herd are condemned to be merely statements of fact such as: 'It's raining', or 'Walter Scott is the author of *Waverley*' (Bertrand Russell took out a patent on this one), or 'My broom is in the corner' (patented by Ludwig Wittgenstein). An anthroposophical truth of this kind might be: 'Doctor Steiner said that truth is a free product of the human spirit.' Well and good. But only a little grain of scholastic logic would suffice to unmask this sentence as an *untruth* in the mouth of one whose mind is intent only on

---

*R. Steiner, *Goethe the Scientist* (GA 1), tr. O.D. Wannamaker (New York, Anthroposophic Press, 1950).

imitating *someone else's* free products. *Heuristically* Rudolf Steiner's anthroposophy belongs to us all, but *existentially* no one can become an anthroposophist who has not come to grips with his *own* 'philosophy of freedom' and fought his way to the threshold of the spiritual world 'by the armour of righteousness on the right hand and on the left' (2 Cor. 6,7). Failing this we shall be in danger of remaining for ever asylum seekers and alms recipients at Steiner's door, a vast horde of eternal descendents claiming someone else's inheritance under false pretences.

We would do well to face up to the answer ourselves: Has anthroposophical truth become individual truth for each one of us, *by name!* wherever we try to exorcise our own mediocrity while drifting with the whim of our oh! so significant destiny? If the answer is Yes, then I shall say no more. If No … but have I not recently spoken about this very 'No' in calling this book the *least* read of the century, even though participants in seminars especially devoted to it have read it to bits? Whatever the case may be, let us remember: It is down to us to save it as it stands helpless on our bookshelves, in the hope that a time will come when it will at last be read, experienced, lived-through, lived-by, what am I saying! — *eaten up.*

## 2. Abstention from all logic by the conscious mind

Here is a question of the first importance: *How* are we supposed to read *The Philosophy of Freedom*? Without any doubt this stylistically harmonious and not in the least conspicuous book calls for an unusual reading method. The first obstacle to be overcome is the very harmony of style already mentioned. A modern reader (whether in 1893 or 1993), accustomed to treating a good read as a *show*, and mistaking a book for a rodeo offering cheap thrills rather than understanding, will find *The Philosophy of Freedom* to be an utter flop. No trace of a doping scandal emerges in this perhaps most *anti-Tristanesque* book ever written. To get an idea of the uniqueness of this work by Steiner you have to imagine the whole of Nietzsche's argumentation stated in a decidedly *contra-Nietzschean* manner.

Remarkably, the fundamental epistemological premise of *The Philosophy of Freedom* appears as though impressed upon its style: the entire book is executed in a way that makes it appear (for *us*, its readers) like *a semi-real* book, of which the full and final reality can only be achieved by our comprehension of it. Hence our very first exercise is to learn to read it in a fitting manner, which means while standing on our own two feet. There was nothing that Rudolf Steiner observed more strictly or stressed more energetically when speaking about *The Philosophy of Freedom* than this condition: *Learn to think independently.* For (and I am here paraphrasing the argument of a lecture he gave to the workers at the Goetheanum) people today are quite incapable of thinking.

The reason for this is that modern thinking has been formed by the Latin language, a language that has a specific peculiarity: it thinks for itself. So when people today assume they are thinking, it is, in fact, not they who are thinking but the Latin language that is thinking in them and through them, even if they don't know any Latin—for it is not the letter of Latin but the spirit of Latin that permeates our entire educational system.

'People are quite right when they say: The brain thinks. Why does the brain think? Because Latin syntax goes into the brain and the brain thinks quite automatically ... Automatons of the Latin language go about in the world without thinking for themselves at all.' 'That is why ... it became necessary for me to write the book about a philosophy of freedom. It is not the contents of *The Philosophy of Freedom* that are so important, though obviously at the time I did wish to tell the world what is said in it; the most important thing is that independent thinking appeared in this book for the first time. No one can possibly understand this book who does not think independently ... When this book appeared ... people didn't know at all what to make of it. It was as if someone in Europe wrote Chinese and no one could understand it. It was written in German, but people were completely unaccustomed to the thoughts expressed in it.'* For 'there is everywhere a kind of fear of ... active thinking, and hence people find it so hard to come to grips with something that demands that they think actively, such as my *Philosophy of Freedom*. The book contains thoughts that are different from those they are accustomed to nowadays, so when they read it some of them stop again quite soon for the simple reason that they are trying to read it as though it were an ordinary book. To read an ordinary book, people settle down on their *chaise-longue*, lean back, thus becoming almost entirely passive,

---

*R. Steiner, *Learning to see into the Spiritual World—Lectures to the Workers at the Goetheanum* (in GA 350), tr. W. Stuber and M. Gardner (New York, Anthroposophic Press, 1990).

and let the thoughts pass before them in procession ... However, what I have attempted to portray in my *Philosophy of Freedom* cannot be read in this fashion because you have to keep on pulling yourself together in order not to be sent to sleep by the thoughts it contains. It is insufficient merely to sit on the *chaise-longue,* and lean back if you like, because once you have quietened your external body you have to set the whole of you, your inner being of soul and spirit, in motion so that your thinking can also begin to move. If you fail to do this you will fall asleep, as indeed many do; and these are more honest than some. The most dishonest are those who read *The Philosophy of Freedom* as though it were an ordinary book and then believe they have genuinely followed its train of thought. In fact they have done no such thing, for they have merely translated the words, which are like husks. They read the words without extracting what only emerges from the words when they are struck as when the steel strikes the flint in the tinderbox.'*

So: *Learn to think independently.* That means: Seek contact with your own thinking; enter into a direct experience of it; sound it out as you sound out the most delicate nuances in your own inner life. Let's leave on one side any kind of learning or education and endeavour to understand the crucial thing by simply paying proper attention and applying our ordinary common sense to it.

What do we actually do when we imagine we are thinking? At best we logically and expertly combine terms and concepts; at worst we merely string words together. We may leave aside the worst cases, even though they are the most numerous, on the assumption that it is best to base one's judgements on the better examples than on

---

*R. Steiner, *Der Goetheanismus—ein Umwandlungsimpuls und Auferstehungsgedanke* (GA 188), Dornach 1982, lecture of 5 January 1919.

the worst (however numerous these may be). So we will take the better examples, the so-called professional thinkers, as our yardstick; and we discover a very instructive and very scandalous state of affairs: It is possible for an individual to write numerous scholarly books in which looking for a single thought is like hunting for a needle in a haystack.

Light can be shed on this scandal by investigating what led up to it. We must assume that future 'thinkers', before they become teachers, have themselves undergone an apprenticeship in which they learnt, in the main, the *logic* or the *grammar* of thinking. There are rules that make the combination of a feminine adjective form with a masculine noun improper, for example. Similarly certain rules forbid the proof of something by means of that which is to be proved. So now the future 'thinker', having learnt the ABC of thinking, sets out to play the games—the philosophical doctrines, views, systems—that have been played already. The grammar expands into taxonomy and the relevant classifications. All the games learnt can be grouped under such headings as 'rationalism', 'empiricism', 'materialism', 'idealism', and so on. Stereotyped oppositions are set up: 'subjective—objective', 'reality—appearance', 'concept—percept', in short, nothing but 'black boxes' about which judgements can be formed in accordance with parameters that are *input* and *output*, but of which the *content* remains unfathomable.

Today's comprehension of thinking as a 'black box' of this nature is one of those epoch-making philosophical and scientific idiocies that are taken for granted nowadays and to which even John Locke brilliantly bore witness—in so very English a manner—when he set out to explain the mechanism of thinking: 'And since the extension, figure, number and motion of bodies of an observable bigness may be perceived ... by the sight, it is evident some singly imperceptible bodies must come from them to the eyes, and thereby convey to the brain some motion; which produces these ideas which we have of them in us.'*

The mathematician Henri Poincaré once compared this view of thinking with that apocryphal machine in Chicago into one end of which live piglets were stuffed while out of the other hams and sausages emerged. What happens in between is a purely technical matter. The only important thing is to grasp the various philosophers' terms and concepts and combine them in a new way, without overstepping the bounds of the combinatorial process. It is considered entirely normal that no experience of the content of the thoughts is involved and that the only important thing is the correct combination of the technical terms. A chess-player would laugh in the face of someone wanting to talk to him about what a pawn experiences; similarly, a philosopher merely shrugs when asked what an experience of a 'transcendental apperception' is like. To sum up: the thought is reduced to a technical term and this term is explained by means of another term. The term 'thinking' remains in force, of course (in order to preserve the camouflage), but its meaning is reduced to a technical instruction, nothing more.

Let us face the facts. Not every 'thinker', perhaps, would have the gall to define the thought process in the words once used by a mathematician when asked what he actually did: 'I merely define certain symbols, and then I explain the rules of how to combine them; that is all.'† That is, indeed, all, and by implying in this manner that *'that is all'* there is to thinking, philosophy again and again merely documents its own unsoundness. (In parenthesis, is this not perhaps

---

*John Locke, *An Essay Concerning Human Understanding*, (London, Fontana Library, 1960, p. 113).
† For, says Poincaré, 'there is no need at all for the mathematician to understand what he is doing' (Henri Poincaré, *Science and Method*, London, 1914).

the reason why it became possible, from a certain point in history onwards, to poke fun at and indeed belabour philosophers, as happens in one of Molière's immortal scenes? Plato, Plotinus, Bonaventura—what bourgeois low-brow would ever have thought of mocking them in antiquity or the Middle Ages?)

Sound common sense, thank goodness, remains indestructible, so for every educated 'combination expert' we can surely find an intelligent derider who may not be much good at reading and writing but will always muster a healthy sneeze at what Goethe once called 'verbal rubbish'. The most startling such 'sneeze' occurred during the first meeting between Goethe and Schiller when they conversed about the 'archetypal plant', an encounter that Rudolf Steiner described as *defining the essence of that period in world history*. Goethe, the autodidact, spoke about 'experience', whereupon Schiller countered: 'That is not an experience, it's an idea.' Like a flash of lightning summarizing the whole of the fifth post-Atlantean era came Goethe's reply: '*It follows, then, that I am seeing the idea.*'

What an astonishing scene! It might well be described as the all-embracing *archetypal phenomenon* of the history of philosophy. Schiller, the educated Kantian scholar, failed entirely to enter into the essence of what was being said. The 'transcendental subject' in him, or more appropriately, the 'automaton of the Latin language', quite automatically registered the contravention of the rule. *Experience* and *idea* were being confused, but it was not permitted to confuse them—'*that is all*'. What would we say of a grammar school teacher—poor innocent soul—who went through Hegel's *Phenomenology of Mind* with a red pencil in his hand as though it were no more than a schoolboy's essay! Goethe—no less innocent, indeed *innocent* in his very greatness—who hadn't the faintest idea about any rules (his beneficial destiny having preserved him from a philosophical education), Goethe instinctively went to the core of the matter in a manner appropriate to its nature by simply describing his *experience* and treating it as just that. This is where the dilemma arises. Either we learn the correct combinations and stick firmly to one thing being the 'experience' and the other the 'idea', which would entail taking leave of oneself and switching one's *own* thinking over to autopilot. Or: To the devil with all rules if they contradict my own sound experience, which results in Galileo's wonderfully defiant: 'But it does move!', or, in Goethe's version: 'It follows, then, that I am seeing the idea.' Yes, I see it myself, with my very own eyes ('He sees at every pore,' said Emerson about Goethe) and no terminological 'cataract' shall blur my vision. For: Even if someone were to prove mathematically the advisability of relying on other people's words rather than on my own eyes, I would still prefer in every circumstance to keep my eyes open and firmly block my ears.

A charming anecdote from a Parisian salon at the time of the Enlightenment encapsulates this entire controversy. A gentleman, discovering his fiance *in flagrante delicto*, begins to upbraid her, paying no attention whatever to her excuses and declarations of misunderstanding. Finally she bitterly opines: 'I see now, my dear, that you love me no longer, for you would rather believe your eyes than my words.'

(A question, in parenthesis to avoid being led astray by the possibilities of this theme: Did Goethe *the dilettante* really break the rules by combining 'experience' and 'idea', and was the incomparable friend who reprimanded him, and who in this point stood *under the influence of Latin*, actually right? Goethe's truth—however instinctive it might have been—was founded not only on an experience of the original beginnings of philosophy, since forgotten, from the pre-Socratics right up to the Platonists of Chartres, but also on the semantics of the Greek language in which 'idea' means literally 'that which is visible'. Behind Schiller, on the other hand, stood academic tradition and His A Priori Highness, Kant.)

The alternatives open to us can be formulated with crystal clarity: We have to choose between *independent* thinking and the non-thinking that functions in us *without any effort on our part*, in other words between a thinking that can be an individual experience and a 'thinking' reduced to a mere technique, which (as Husserl aptly put it) is not essentially different from playing cards or chess.* In keeping with the resounding box on the ear once administered by Meister Eckhart ('If none had come I should have been obliged to preach to this poor-box'), I have to say that *The Philosophy of Freedom* is designed exclusively for the former. *To read this book means to bring it forth again from one's own experience; it means: to become it.* 'Thinkers' who sink into the cushioned comfort of the latter and thus contra-indicate their inner self have nothing to look for in it.

Once again we come up against the question: How is one to read this book? By cultivating independent thinking, it demands of its readers that same capacity. This can only mean that we must make suitable preparation beforehand, and such preparation can be found in another book of Steiner's: *Truth and Knowledge*, published immediately before *The Philosophy of Freedom* and bearing the sub-title 'Prelude to a Philosophy of Freedom'.† This prelude is epistemological, and its central concern—achievement of *freedom from assumptions* by means of a radical clear-out from our minds of all the ballast of passively and mechanically acquired knowledge with which we are

---

*Edmund Husserl, *The Crisis of European Sciences and Transcendental Philosophy* (Evanston, Northwestern University Press, 1970).
†R. Steiner, *Truth and Knowledge. An Introduction to The Philosophy of Spiritual Activity* (GA 3), tr. R. Stebbing (New York, Steinerbooks, 1981).

weighed down*—brings us to the point at which an adequate comprehension of *The Philosophy of Freedom* is achievable.

Let us look once more at the example cited above in the hope of reaching a real understanding of what is meant. Goethe, having no particular concern with rules of any kind, described to Schiller his *experience* which indeed proved to be *supersensible*. Schiller objected that he had confused experience and idea. Goethe's starting point was not a technical term but his personal experience, for which he subsequently discovered a pertinent term (the 'archetypal plant'). For Schiller the starting point was the term, which meant that he used terminology to prescribe what the experience ought to be. The terms in question are 'experience' and 'idea'. According to the rules of modern philosophy the 'idea' must on no account be the subject of 'experience' but 'experience' may be permitted to carry out an attack on the 'idea'. People adhered to the following rule: Experience was always *sensible* experience, whereas the idea was *supersensible*, exercising in cognition not a *constitutive* but a *regulative* role (a 'public opinion' of pure reason which exercised moral control from above on the categorial nature of what is given through the senses).

---

* A few decades later this procedure generated the voluminous literature of *phenomenology*. All on his own, Husserl embarked on the ultimate heroic attempt of protecting philosophy against the enervation of positivism, endeavouring to think radically right back to its original beginnings. This is not the place for a discussion of the various misfortunes of this astonishing endeavour, which enabled that strictest of logicians among other things to get exceedingly close to the question of *reincarnation*, after which he had to admit his inability to make a further *logical* step. Let it merely be said: Not only have phenomenologists yet to discover Steiner in order to become truly radical in their search for the first principle; anthroposophists, conversely, still need to discover Husserl if they want to see how it was possible to tread Steiner's path philosophically without knowing or, in all probability, wanting to know (what a tragic paradox!) anything about Steiner.

Cognition, i.e. the reasoned thought, is always directed downwards (towards sense-given experience).* Should it dare to direct itself upwards, this means, according to Kant, that it has succumbed to the temptation of the worst kind of *transcendental illusion* and relinquished scientific authenticity in favour of metaphysical charlatanism.†

We now have to ask: Why do the 'health police' have to impose these rules? Why has experience been banished to the zone of the purely sensible? Why must it confine itself to statements such as: 'Here is a candle-stick, and here is a snuff-box' (as Hegel once devastatingly characterized Kantian experience)?‡ Who granted that notary of reason the right to declare as charlatans those who are gifted *by nature* with a capacity to think that is free-as-a-bird rather than buried under the ground. Does the mole have the right to criticize the eagle and deny it reality?

When Wittgenstein and many others later described philosophy as a 'sickness of language' this went to the heart of the problem (never mind any nihilistic disadvantages of that diagnosis). It was indeed a sickness of language, a mush of unchewed concepts and categories, an addling of the brain, nothing but terminological looseness of the bowel. What other dietary cure but great frugality can the physician prescribe in such a case! Avoidance of dogmatic terms and judgements, wholesale abstention from all logic by the conscious mind, for the very reason that it wants to be just that—'conscious in its existence'—and not some

---

*Christian Morgenstern conducted his own physical experiment to test this Kantian rule: 'It is an odd sensation to send your thoughts vertically downwards into the earth beneath your feet. You don't get very far; imagination is literally suffocated.' Morgenstern, *Stufen* (Munich, 1922, p. 47).

†Fanciers of unlikely analogies will recognize in this the genealogy of Orwell's 'thought police'.

‡Hegel, 'Vorlesungen über die Geschichte der Philosophie III', *Gesammelte Werke* (Frankfurt/Main, 1971, p. 352).

penny-in-the-slot machine inexhaustibly spewing out terminological combinations for its colleagues (sorry!—its fellow vending machines). If this could be achieved it would amount to that freedom from assumptions realized in the *prelude* to *The Philosophy of Freedom*.

To use an analogy: Let's talk of transferring the practice of asceticism from the bodily realm to thinking, not as an end in itself but as a prophylactic therapy. Modern epistemologists are hermits of thinking, purifying it from customary terminological lasciviousness; and in this point Steiner's theory of knowledge proves itself to be, refined and carried into the sphere of pure logic, the practice described in the old hagiographies. To develop the analogy further: Wooed by a plethora of terms and concepts, thinking makes its choice as did the young Francis of Assisi—it opts for *poverty*, *La Povertà*. In such a context even the biblical saying 'Blessed are the poor in spirit' can be given an *epistemological* interpretation.

To put it plainly: I don't know the meaning of 'experience' nor of 'idea', nor, now that a chain reaction has been set in motion, of any of those philosophical terms I absorbed at university: outer and inner, subjective and objective, reality and appearance, chance and necessity, cause, end, thing-in-itself, free will, matter, spirit, soul, body, substance and accident, apperception. I provisionally disenfranchise all of this, not because I question its significance but because I intend to think it *for myself* and consequently won't permit such learning to make a fool of me or declare me a genius (depending on whether I am in or out of luck). So now my mind simply ceases to be a passive screen across which flash various combinations of concepts and ideas while I am relegated to the role of a competent technician who has merely plugged in to the 'philosophic' circuit. The condition is clearly stated: Not one of the concepts listed above will be permitted to enter my purified consciousness until I have gained *an experience that substantiates it*. That is the only rule I must adhere to if I intend to think *independently* rather than because I happen to have been taught philosophy. Only then can philosophy cease to be a sickness of language and become genuine cognition.

Naturally I'm not suggesting that we should stick to this rule with the narrow-minded pedantry of a splitter of hairs. It will be broken in one way or another at almost every step of the path as we struggle to achieve the quickening of thinking. But where deviation is impossible to avoid, it is important to remember: Although from time to time I have to use a term or form a judgement for which *as yet* I have no basis in experience, nevertheless I do so with my eyes open and because I cannot avoid it; I do it *heuristically*, on tick, you might say, against future experience, and also in the hope of evoking such experience. This is the point at which the *How* of *The Philosophy of Freedom* coincides with the *What*. We are already absorbing its content when we learn to read it in an adequate manner. This is perhaps also a reliable way of making a beginning at learning how to receive and welcome its unfathomable *Who* at some time long hence, perhaps millennia ahead.

## 3. Thinking: the eye of the needle

The fundamental keynote of the book is struck in its sub-title: 'Some results of introspective observation following the methods of natural science.' Superficially this appears to hold up a mildly critical mirror to Eduard von Hartmann's *The Philosophy of the Unconscious* with its sub-title: 'Speculative results obtained by the inductive methods of science.' Von Hartmann—the most brilliant thinker of the nineteenth century, as Rudolf Steiner once called him—was the young Steiner's main opponent and perhaps, indeed, his most outstanding 'Latin *doppelgänger*'. In this regard, and against this background, *The Philosophy of Freedom* was written as a philosophy of the *conscious* (polemics against von Hartmann, both overt and covert, continue over many pages). What is the basis for the difference, or should we say the enharmonic change, between the sub-titles of these two books? Above all the necessity to be in tune with the epistemological trends of the time. From the second half of the nineteenth century onwards the *scientific* approach has played a solo tune in the concert of world views. To leave it out of consideration in favour of the skills of long since outmoded metaphysical or mystical contemplation would have meant turning one's back entirely on the rhythms of historical change. That was the one side. On the other it was becoming increasingly obvious that this kind of cognition had a dangerous tendency to get stuck in materialistic interpretations. A scientific type was growing ever more common, a researcher capable of making *marvellous* discoveries and following these up with *deplorable* interpretations (Haeckel is a case in point). Externally, in the popular view, these interpretations appeared so nearly identical with the discoveries that scarcely any doubt remained as to their organic unity. An unavoidable choice between two wrongs arose: that of harnessing science to the yoke of materialism, or that of rejecting materialism and thus maltreating science at the same time. On this point the watershed between 'university' and *'vie de bohème'* split cultural life as a whole into two rival factions powerlessly vying with one another: that of the pig-headed 'physicists' and that of the addle-pated 'lyricists'.

One thing was definite: the battle for scientific knowledge turned out to be *the battle for the spirit*, in which the spirit would either deepen the data of scientific materialism to the point at which a new approach to spiritual life would be achieved (not a poetic but a scientific spirituality), or get stuck in these data and thus draw the pathological conclusion that it was itself the most supremely organized matter. This is what is meant by the orientation towards the 'scientific method' in von Hartmann's sub-title as well as in Steiner's: the form of the thoughts and the train of thinking are strictly in accordance with the empirical procedure of scientific research. The divergence only arises at the level of the *content*.

Von Hartmann subjects empirical observation to speculation, to the purely a priori way of thinking, to the assumption-laden thinking that now proceeds to work on *physical* data with the same existential alienation previously applied to *metaphysical* data (by Descartes, for example, or Spinoza). Steiner, on the other hand, observes the *inner life*, or the purely inward experience of thinking, which can quite well be described in a scientific manner. This method is highly original, not only in its novelty but also in its existential reliability. Perhaps we can immediately grasp its uniqueness with the help of two rather unexpected analogies.

Imagine Galileo transferring his attention from the free fall of a solid body to his own thought processes. Imagine him doing this in a *purely Galileian* manner, taking not the slightest notice of any Kantian ticking-off, just as he took no notice of the ticking-off he got from the Schoolmen when he allowed the object to reveal its own nature.* Or imagine Meister Eckhart suddenly turning in one of his sermons from the theme of profundity and silence to that of the law of biogenesis, and therefore changing his style and manner of discussion to suit the new subject.

In his later book on mysticism Steiner formulated this most forcefully: 'Only one who understands the spirit in the sense of *true* mysticism can gain a full understanding of facts in the physical world.' And also: 'Meister Eckhart as well as Tauler, and Jacob Boehme as well as Angelus Silesius, would experience the deepest satisfaction in contemplating this science. The spirit in which *they* sought to regard the world has passed in the fullest sense into this conception of the physical world *if it is properly understood* ... It is true that today there are many who think that accepting the "facts" discovered by science without further ado is tantamount to falling into a shallow, dry materialism. I myself stand completely upon the ground of modern science. I am convinced that with a conception of nature such as that of Ernst Haeckel, only those can become shallow who approach it with a world of ideas that is already shallow. I feel something higher and more glorious when I enter into the *revelations* of his *History of Creation* than when I

---

*Perhaps this is where we should look for the cause of all the later misfortunes of Husserl's phenomenology which had sought from the beginning—entirely in Steiner's sense—to be termed the theory of 'logical experiences' but which had preferred to find its orientation not in the scientific method but in the tradition of the Schoolmen. This is where Husserl was held back by the warning calls of the unassailed *Guardian of the Threshold*. While the young Steiner's experience with Brentano was nothing more than a *personal* salute to a glorious shade of the past, in Husserl's case the matter became a pointer along the way; it was a tragically futile attempt to grasp hold of the future by means of cast-offs from medieval Aristotelianism.

am confronted with the stories of supernatural miracles told in various creeds. I know of nothing in any "holy writ" that reveals to me anything as sublime as the "dry" fact that, in the womb, every human embryo briefly goes through all the forms through which its animal ancestors have evolved.'*

Note that the man who says this has already sacrificed the life of an independent writer, untrammelled by any external constraints, for the sake of theosophical *commitment*.† The exceptional sharpness of these markedly challenging and indeed markedly incautious formulations is merely an artifice in imitation of Nietzsche's recent majestic testing of Stendhal's maxim about making one's entry into society with a duel. Those of us, if any, who are still capable of comprehending what it must have meant for the author of *The Philosophy of Freedom* to become a member of the Theosophical Society, an action—let there be no doubt about this—on which he depended for the sake of that book, so that it should make its way into the world instead of remaining 'the experience of a lone individual',‡ will find this sharpness not only tactically justified but in fact the only way. It was a matter (to continue even more sharply) of letting those long-haired, pious devotees and conspirators of Himalayan secrets, future 'uncles' and 'aunties' in the Anthroposophical Society, know in no uncertain terms WHOM exactly they were about to follow! Behind the tactics, however, the mighty outline of a strategy for the

---

*R. Steiner, *Mysticism at the Dawn of the Modern Age* (GA 7), tr. K.E. Zimmer (New York, Steinerbooks, 1980).

† *The Philosophy of Freedom*, with its promise of an entirely fresh esoteric approach, proved unheard to such an extent that it became necessary to clean out the Augean stable of theosophy before the foundation stone of the future Goetheanum could be laid.

‡ It may need stating even more emphatically about his later entry into the Anthroposophical Society—so shortly before his death: that this, too, was necessary, still for the same reason.

future began to emerge: 'Some results of introspective observation following the methods of natural science', where the introspective mind, in following the methods of science, would no longer slither into a trance of mystical sensations, and where the plain facts of science, logically interpreted in terms of the inner life, would lead to the illumination of spiritual experience.

'And ye shall know the truth, and the truth shall make you free.' The book is structured according to these most profound words of the Redeemer; each of its two parts follows this through consistently: 'Ye shall know the truth' ('Knowledge of Freedom'), and 'the truth shall make you free' ('The Reality of Freedom'). For only *truth* leads to *freedom*. Over centuries of traditional philosophy the problem of 'free will' had been talked to death and ended up in the unavoidable cul-de-sac of philosophical aporia. Now it turns out to be another sickness of language. *Will* has pushed *thinking* aside, so that philosophers, instead of discussing the *freedom of thinking,* have clung instead to the spectre of a *free will*. But the will is *not* free, or rather, its freedom can only be achieved through a freeing of thinking from the slag of sense-perception so that the two can reach an ultimate identification in which thinking is no longer separate from will, when both unite as the *thinking-in-will* and *will-in-thinking* of the whole human being's thoughts and actions.

Let us say it now, to anticipate the analysis we shall be undertaking: A *reality of freedom* unpenetrated with a *knowledge of freedom* risks becoming anything *but* freedom based on truth. For freedom perceived as will disinfected of forcibly administered conventions is quite simply a pseudo-freedom that liberates human beings from moral slavery only to harness them to the yoke of their instincts. The liberation of the will, i.e. of obscure unconscious elements, is synonymous with the seizure of power by chaos and despotism. Genuine freedom does not set in until *thinking* is liberated. The one and only eye of the needle through which the perspectives of human freedom can open up turns out to be thinking. 'You shall know the truth' means: You shall take possession of your thoughts so that thinking becomes your guide on the way to the truth which alone *will set you free*.

This now becomes the very first thing we recognize in the science of freedom: in thinking we depend not one jot on the external world (including our own physiology, which is a part of that external world). Everything else—our entire given world picture—we receive from the outside, through our senses; thinking is the *only* thing that is autonomously given, without any subjugation to physical or psychological processes. This basic tenet of German idealism is brought back to life here in the dimension of the *theory of knowledge*. For the tragic fate of that idealism, bewitched by the ontological and metaphysical building of thought-castles in the air, was that it unconditionally left the *epistemological* foundation to *Kantianism* which found no difficulty in showing that the gravitational laws of that foundation permitted of no autonomy in thinking and in hinting that thinking only becomes feasible through being bound to the sense-perceptible world.

*The Philosophy of Freedom* follows to its conclusion *epistemologically* the line of German idealism and—which is especially important—it does this not only within the framework of *logic*\* but also *scientifically*, i.e. *experimentally* and *empirically*. This is the very nub of the matter. We are told that it is not the conception, the thought itself, that is autonomous but our recognition *through experience* of this autonomy; our first recognition of the thought is not a

---

\* As for example in Hermann Cohen's *Logic of Pure Thought*. Masterly in its execution, it nevertheless in the final analysis boils down to the feeble artifice of correcting Kant by means of Hegel, a Hegel, however, who has already been revised by Kant.

dogmatic a priori experience but an experience in the direct, empirical sense of the word, and because the nature of the object being recognized is not sense-perceptible the experience itself is *supersensible*. This leads perfectly clearly to the rule that we must not *dispute* but *examine*. All objections voiced by 'qualified' philosophers against *The Philosophy of Freedom* are doomed to absurdity so long as they are founded on the empty clatter of the rationalistic rattle rather than the empirical certainty of individual experience.

In fact, the motto later attached to Steiner's collected works suits this case in the highest degree: 'The right to form a judgement about the content of *The Philosophy of Freedom* can only be conceded to those familiar with the accepted conditions on which such judgement must be founded.' And this can only mean: *Those who have entirely absorbed in mind and spirit the freedom it has achieved*. How else is one to cope with those hosts of educated parasites who, shameless and without conscience as they are, remain so set on not confining themselves to their own intellectual feats. 'When my *Philosophy of Freedom* appeared,' Steiner remembered later, 'I was as much in need of an opinion on it as any ignorant beginner. I received one from a gentleman whose only reason for writing books was probably the existence of innumerable volumes by other authors—which he had not understood. He informed me most thoughtfully that I would have noticed my mistakes if I "had gone more deeply into psychological, logical, and epistemological studies"; and he proceeded to enumerate all the books that I should read in order to become as clever as he: "Mill, Sigwart, Wundt, Riehl, Paulsen, B. Erdmann." '*

Positivism props up thinking with the crutches of sense-

---

*R. Steiner, *Mysticism at the Dawn of the Modern Age*, op. cit.

perceptibility because in its mania for facts it dogmatically reduces experience to sense-perceptible data. Yet it is the very nature of the Critical Philosophy not to accept anything as real that cannot pass the border control of the conscious mind. This Critical Philosophy, smothered by Kant in countless compromises and dogmatic flirtations, was not truly realized until Steiner produced his phenomenology of thinking. We are not strictly empirical unless we stop limiting experience in any way whatsoever but instead place our trust in it and test it by means of our own sound capacity to judge. We then discover that our experience has many levels or is, we might say, *hierarchical*. The first level of experience is simply the fact of direct perception without any categorizing of what is perceived. (Remember: we have a provisional veto against concepts because of their being not yet in our awareness.) The merely given in perception, however, is chaos. We cannot yet talk of knowledge at this level; the thing that is present is *the will to gain knowledge*.

For: Conscious thinking (as opposed to merely intellectual thought) does not *exist*, it *becomes*, and as something in the process of becoming it is always *voluntaristic* and *imperativistic* (this would be the proper location in which to seek the genesis of the categorical imperative, most humbly stolen from cognition by Kant and presented to morality) and never in any situation passive or discursive. In other words in thinking, knowledge is affected by *the will*, or, more exactly and concretely, by an archetypal demiurgic 'fiat!'. In the context of this level of experience, where discursiveness—lacking any right to be an a priori concept—has nothing to do with the empiricism of sense-perceptible data, one can only speak of such a 'fiat!' as applying to knowledge itself, for knowledge would not come into existence without it. To stick with experience means not to stray beyond the framework of given fact. But the given facts of our direct perception of the world are, without exception, chaotic.

Then we ask ourselves: Can we discover anything among these given facts that can provide a starting point for cognition. For so long as we merely stare passively at the given facts, cognition cannot begin. It cannot begin until we find within the given fact a *higher* given fact, the fact of *thought,* and when this appears our experience widens qualitatively to embrace the supersensible. We then realize that a concept is not an empty categorial form of Kantian analysis but the form through which the content of the world flows into us. Cognition then becomes the union of the two halves of given fact, the union of pure perception with pure concept, because in addition to the given fact of sense experience we discover the corresponding given fact of supersensible experience (i.e. of thought).

In Kant's account of the synthesis, through the categories, of purely formal concepts with the content of sense-experience we are confronted with a caricature of the act of cognition. Drawn as a cartoon this caricature might appear as follows: The sense perception comes *from* things (*in-themselves*) *to* the head, while the conceptual form goes *from* the head *to* the things (in accordance with the doctrines of the Transcendental Aesthetic). The spiteful mischief of the ancient Eleatic tortoise ever and again forces cognition to play tricks with logic: for, the Achilles-head (otherwise thought to be the heel), having met with an accident, is in no way destined to catch up with the unrecognizable tortoises of things.

When the head relies on experience instead of scholarly tradition it breaks away from this trance-like state and realizes: The form situated *in* it is merely the husk of a thought (an empty Kantian 'concept'); the thought itself is situated *in* the thing as its *nature* and *meaning,* and the single task of cognition is to extract it *from* the thing and then *grasp* the thing with it by finding a suitable concept for it.*

However, the mere act of 'extracting' is still not cognition. The content of the world still appears chaotic because it is not yet *grasped*, it has not yet been linked with a concept. Only thinking can give meaning and order to the content; direct perception gives us merely its sense-perceptible (its unrecognized) side: the world travelling *incognito*.

From this perspective arises the wondrous *experience* of *The Philosophy of Freedom*, an experience we have never had before: WHEN WE THINK, WE ARE IN THE UNIVERSE. This experience is pregnant with the whole rainbow palette of future *wise* occultism. For (let us say it yet again): If the thought reduced to a concept and the concept reduced to an empty a priori container were to content themselves, if you will pardon my saying so, with a 'navel-contemplating' cognition, then the philosophers, whose task it would be to represent the rights of pure reason in this impure game, would find themselves wrestling to discover a solution to a contradictory rebus which—in all seriousness—would be worthy of a decidedly *psychiatric* intervention. If the thing is situated *outside* the head and the thought *inside* it, how can it ever be possible for the thought to step *out of* the head and *into* the thing? It goes without saying that only the mystical 'navel' (clothed in respectable categorical garments such as 'empathy' or '*élan vital*' to preserve the supposed reputation

---

*Almost more than anywhere else Goethe's maxim proves opportune here: 'One should write little, but draw much.' Drawing would be capable of defending cognition against maltreatment by bungling words. Steiner once said the same with reference, astonishingly, to *The Philosophy of Freedom*: 'I would draw the content of my *Philosophy of Freedom*. This would not be hard to do. Only no one would be able to interpret it nowadays, because in our time we are trained to react to "words".' (From the lecture 'Wesen und Bedeutung der illustrativen Kunst', Dornach, 3 December 1917, published by Section for the Arts at the Goetheanum.)

of the Academy) would be capable of accomplishing such a trick. The thought—hopelessly estranged from the world and shut up inside the head—would in any case become superfluous.

It appears that no appeal was possible against David Hume's conclusion: '... let us chase our imagination to the heavens, or to the utmost limits of the universe; we never really advance a step beyond ourselves, nor can conceive any kind of existence, but those perceptions, which have appeared in that narrow compass.'* The answer given by *The Philosophy of Freedom* is decidedly emphatic and clear: All this pathos has nothing whatever to do with the process of thinking. The thought—the *human* alias the *cosmic* (as we shall see later)—is in its pristine state *outside* us and *in* the universe. We repeat, in order to avoid any possible misunderstanding: the THOUGHT; not its conceptual husk of words.

The most decisive question of all confronts us herewith: What is the relationship of *this* thought with *us*? or: What are *we* expected to do with *it*? Traditional epistemology pays no particular attention to this question since it is presumed that the thought appearing in the act of cognition is, of all things, *our* thought. The democratic pronoun 'we' as employed by Hume or Kant may be taken in the same vein. This alarming and anonymous 'we', which has the effrontery to assume competence as the *subject of the cognition*, now emerges as the obstacle over which all theories of knowledge have hitherto fatally stumbled and to which they owe their limping gait.

It is permissible to ask with every emphasis who is meant by this 'we'. It goes without saying that *we* are all *equal* before the law. The questionable merit of the *philosopher* Francis Bacon provides no guarantee of favours for the

---

*David Hume, *A Treatise of Human Nature*, Book One (Fontana Library, London, 1962, p. 113).

*statesman* Francis Bacon when caught committing bribery. There is, however, nothing more nonsensical or wicked than applying this equality also in matters of cognition. Read once again Hume's conclusion quoted above; or consider the uncountable passages in which Kant speaks in *our* name ('our experience', 'our understanding', 'our cognition', etc.). Ask yourself what 'we' they are talking about. This 'we' of Kant and Hume can, of course, encompass certain types of thinker with ease—let's make a random count: a Newton, a Locke, a Jean Jacques Rousseau with all his admirers, male and female, the Encyclopaedists, the heroes in novels by a Rétif de la Bretonne, old Lampe (Kant's faithful famulus), and, it goes without saying, Kant himself. Obviously, even with the best will in the world, we could not include in this list a Plato, a Goethe or a Swedenborg, let alone any bon vivant or riotous character, or even Wolfgang Köhler's intelligent chimps, so clever at tracking down the principles of *Gestalt*.

It is not with the legalistically generalized 'we' that cognition commences, but with the 'I' alone, though again not with any and every 'I' when it appears merely as a constraint of grammar (like another 'we'), but with the *exclusive* 'I'. Everyone knows that the 'I' of music is called Bach or Mozart or Beethoven or Bruckner, and that the 'I' of painting is called Raphael or Dürer or Rembrandt. To date, thank goodness, no claim is laid to 'we' in fields like this. People don't use the phrase 'I create' so indiscriminately, so shamelessly, so tastelessly or with such lack of conscience as they do the unfortunate 'I think', when every recipient of any kind of diploma reserves the right to be called 'I' and to be capable of 'thinking'.

Let us once and for all take into account that the 'I think' of *The Philosophy of Freedom* can in no way be translated into Descarte's *'cogito'*, for it represents no *genus proximum* but a single *differentia specifica* and is thus emphatically *individual*; indeed it represents a *named* individual, so that the name of the author appearing on the title page must be read as one would read Rembrandt's signature in the bottom corner of one of his greatest creations. This fact must be held constantly in the forefront of our awareness (as readers) if for no other reason than that *we* so often and with such lack of concern mistake the event of thinking here described to be *our own* because we cannot get rid of the illusion that the 'subject' of Steiner's theory of knowledge is as transcendental and general as that of the *Critique of Pure Reason*. This accounts for that bizarre impression left by so many anthroposophical books about Steiner's view of cognition. It is as though someone, having had the good fortune to spend some time contemplating, let us say, Rembrandt's *Night Watch*, were all of a sudden to lock himself up in his studio and set about painting it himself. Steady on, dear anthroposophical friends: one doesn't become a god on the spot or at the first attempt by believing one has created *reality* through the mere synthesis of percept and concept!

Let us now ask what it would mean *to create reality* or, speaking synonymously: *to think*? This, surely, is the unique privilege of the author of *The Philosophy of Freedom* from whom *we* are light-years distant, but whom we can approach at any moment *if we desire to know no other career than one in the realm of the impossible.*

We could begin by trying to comprehend the at first shocking meaning of the assertion that the thought is situated *outside us*. Let this be the first step we take in the impossible, for we have been so spoilt, coddled and pampered and have become so arrogant and consequently so irresponsible in the cradle of that now obsolete tradition which insinuatingly made us believe that the thought is situated in our head and is quite simply our very own private property. We now suddenly discover that if our head with its Latin learning and its Protestant attitudes has anything in it at all, then that something is not a thought but rather the conceptual, word-husk of a thought. The thought itself, by affecting our senses, comes to us from outside in the undifferentiated stream of separate perceptions. Popularly speaking we then talk of the *thing* which, after a brief side-glance at our university learning, turns out to be the *thing-in-itself*; for this our scholarly head can find no more fitting word-husk than that disgraceful *ignorabimus* which is not worthy of human consideration. Step by step, wading against the current of our own habits, we still have to comprehend the fact that what confronts us in this is the *world thought* which has been 'thought into' the thing, in whose physical darkness it has become entrapped. Neither the empty word-husk 'thing' nor our empty staring at the mere physicalness of the 'thing' can explain to us what has happened, which is the shattering realization that every material thing is nothing other than a *cross on which the thought is crucified*, and that we ourselves, higher things among things that we are, form no exception, except that we are potentially the only thing in the world whose death is not (not yet!) *clinical*, but *mystical*. There we lie, countless insensible Lazaruses in the grave of our own bodies pretending to know nothing of the one power on which we can count to ensure that the eternal words may find fulfilment: 'And there shall be no more death.' (Rev., 21,4) This it is that appears in Steiner epistemologically as the synthesis of percept and concept. He expressed the unique significance of this, his synthesis, in the following sentences. (They are like hammer blows and may best be characterized by Nietzsche's powerful phrase: 'And it must seem bliss to you to press your hand upon millennia as upon wax'):

'... *I draw from myself what I see in the things as their deepest being. The thoughts I make for myself about the things, these I produce from my own inner being. They nevertheless belong to the things ... The essential being of the things does not therefore come to me from them, but rather from me. My content is their essential being.'*

Cognition, when understood in this way, is nothing other than the *recognition* within which the thought grasps its own *objectivity* as exemplified by the subjective picture of the world before concepts are formed. Or, put more succinctly, the better to capture the crux of the argument: Cognition is at bottom nothing other than *the communion of the thing with its own original essence which is exemplified by this essence expressing itself in conceptual form*. (Or, in religious terms: The thing, having been excommunicated by being declared unknowable, is re-admitted to Communion through being known, and thus returns to itself, to its originally created state.)

Consider the following chain of increasingly complicated analogies: When we endeavour to conceive of an artificially created object (an artefact), we know that in order to conceive of it we only need to conceive of its *consistency*, its *structure*. What, though, is this consistency other than a *thought* made physical in the object (or, stated mythologically: put into it magically, by enchantment), a *thought* belonging to the craftsman who has created the object! The mechanism of a clock, for example, is merely the thought of the *clockmaker* made objective in *the thing*. So to conceive of this thing would mean to think out in the form of a concept the thought realized in it.† Now let us proceed from *artefacts* to *natural* objects. What is involved in conceiving of a stone, a plant, any natural object, by means of thinking? Again: To draw out its essence and therefore the *thought* conceived of

---

*R. Steiner, *Individualism in Philosophy* (in GA 30), tr. W. Lindemann (Spring Valley, Mercury Press, 1989).
† Particularly recommended in this context is Steiner's lecture of 18 January 1909 *Practical Training in Thought* (in GA 108), tr. H. Monges (New York, Anthroposophic Press, 1966).

in it. This time the thought is not a *human* one, as in the case of the clockmaker, but a *cosmic* one, the one we get a nebulous inkling of whenever we speak about the *creative powers of nature*.

At this point I am forced to pause with the suggestion that we take a closer look at this most deceitful of expressions. What are these 'creative powers of nature'—merely an ordinary expression turned cliché? or—*a fact*? Consider the trouble we take to avoid this question as we recline on the *chaise-longue* of comfortable intellectual reasoning and say: 'Well, simply the creative powers of nature—that's all!' But our old friend *'that's all!'* bursts the bubble of our much vaunted epistemological activity, whether we are dilettantes of philosophy or world-famous thinkers (a more than worrying 'or') like the author of the much-extolled *Creative Evolution* who managed to write a scintillating book about evolution without giving any hint of *who* might be bringing about the evolution or *what* it is that's being created. Free and unconditional thinking, baptized in the font of *The Philosophy of Freedom*, is not brought up short even by this experience. With all the reality of a fact experienced, the creative powers of nature prove to be *the creative thoughts of named cosmic hierarchies* manifesting in natural phenomena and thus as something sense-perceptible. This is where the experience of pure thinking coincides with pure mysticism and OCCULT SCIENCE—without any 'navels' or other idiotically puffed-up occult hocus-pocus. At long last traditional occult nomenclatures come into their own, offering us a rich and rare assortment of symbols and technical terms, whether from East or West, from Africa or, for that matter, New Zealand. While he was still in his 'theosophical' period, Rudolf Steiner demonstrated the technique of translating *The Philosophy of Freedom* into traditional theosophical language in a lecture he gave on 9 February 1905: 'In that book, you will find what I have here been describing expressed in the terminology of western philosophy. You will find in it the development from Kama to Manas. I called Ahamkara the "ego", Manas "higher thinking", pure thinking, and the Buddhi, as I didn't at that time point to their origins, "moral imagination".*

We can also picture a different situation, one in which the experience of the thought fails to make it through to a concrete experience of thinking but is brought up short with an insolent yet cowardly *'that's all'*. Imagine a philosopher who is at a standstill, or bogged down, when he happens on a mystical book, for example by Dionysius the Areopagite. 'What rubbish!' he will surely cry after skimming a few pages. Or at best: 'Blessed are they who believe in all these Angeloi, Archangeloi, Archai etc.' His ears, brought up—if not bred—to appreciate ordinary philosophical and scientific concepts, refuse even to listen to such fairy tales (as though he were not one to swoon in admiration at the enchanted stories of mathematical physics with its 'black holes' and time 'going into reverse'). *For him*, without doubt, such things are fairy tales, that's all.

But now imagine him succeeding in de-Kantifying his thinking and giving it an overhaul in the spirit of *The Philosophy of Freedom*. He would then encounter the *creative powers of nature* not as deserters from the realm of knowledge but as an astonishing and *inexpressible* thought experience in which he would recognize the *objective* presence of cosmic beings. Thereupon he would sit up and take notice if he happened upon Dionysius the Areopagite: 'Goodness gracious! This is the very thing that I have experienced in thought without managing to find any suitable philosophical concept for it!'

It is here that philosophy and science are transformed into *spiritual science* which does not in the least contradict the physical experiment but on the contrary deepens it to

---

*R. Steiner, 'Ursprung und Ziel des Menschen', lecture of 9 February 1905 in *Grundbegriffe der Geisteswissenschaft* (GA 53), Dornach, 1981.

the point where it reveals its essence. Here is a paradox which—let us hope—is destined to become a part of 'general knowledge': Every physicist and biologist, every *scientist* unconsciously (quite soberly) practises occultism, or—with a pinch of Molière's salt—*speaks in prose without realizing it*. The only question is whether the level of his thinking, or rather his capacity to think, corresponds with the level of his experimental and theoretical technique. In other words: Does his thinking prefer the initiation path of *The Philosophy of Freedom* to the *chaise-longue of positivism*? If it does, then this, and only this, will constitute the real *victory over materialism* and become the *self-realization of cognition*. If it does not, then occultism, having been driven out by the door, will force its way in again through the window, this time in its most ugly forms. Disconcerted physicists will wail about the 'rudimentary consciousness of corpuscles' while their no less disconcerted biologist colleagues will draw the logical conclusion and apply to join the séances of 'transcendental meditation'...

The chain of analogies continues. Clearly the thought experience discussed so far has had to do with the supersensible basis of the sense-perceptible: here, at last, both halves become one. To imagine a spiritual cause hidden behind the sense-perceptible world, as do the theologians to this day, together with their legitimate materialistic heirs, would mean to regard the Creator of the world as some power or other playing hide-and-seek, in which case the task of cognition (provided it did not appear disguised in some kind of *'ignorabimus'*) would merely be to solve this crossword puzzle by filling in the empty squares with the six-letter 'spirit'-words instead of the five-letter 'sense'-words. Here once and for all a stop has been put to this nonsense. However, experience continues, as we have just said.

The next step is when thinking becomes immersed in *pure spirit*, where the latter is recognized directly and immediately and no longer through its sense-perceptible manifestations. This is the sphere the experience of which is known as a 'trial by air' in occultism. It is no longer possible to lean on the sensible as a manifestation of the supersensible; one has to find support solely in one's own purely mental capacities. Thinking is confronted with the shattering experience of a mirror-image because it no longer recognizes itself in its conceptual form searching for sense-perceptible data, but as an ORGAN OF PERCEPTION. For: Whereas thinking that is turned towards the sense-perceptible world comes up against those perceptions for which it lacks concepts, it feels, as it turns towards the spiritual world, as though it is itself a concept that lacks a corresponding percept. Kant called this region of thinking a *boundary concept*, a limitation, and strictly censured any progress beyond it. This is where fear of the concretely given spirit (not the spirit that is at home in all kinds of empty phrases) emerges in all clarity. For: If cognition is always possible through the synthesis of concept and percept, and if sense-perceptible data involve sense-perceptions, then cognition of the *directly* given spiritual world must require spiritual perceptions. Thought in the *Critique of Pure Reason*, identifying itself with the empty, logical form, turns rigid with fright when confronted with such perceptions; in contrast, the thinking of *The Philosophy of Freedom*, uniting within itself both form and content, yearns for them.

This is where we arrive at the riddle of the faculty that Goethe called 'the perceptive power of thought', a faculty that has been most frequently attacked in the modern positivist tradition. Objections to the *perceptiveness*, i.e. the *intuitiveness*, of thinking generally stemmed from the simple assumption that the thinking, in looking at the object, must at the same time beget that object. In the Kantian sense it was assumed that the thought as such was empty and became filled with the sense-perceptible data. Any endeavours to disregard sense experience and seek a *different kind* of experience were regarded (as we already know) as charlatanism or, as Kant called them elsewhere, 'adventures of ideas'. In the section 'Transcendental Dialectic' of his *Critique of Pure Reason* Kant describes such adventures of ideas, which finally degenerate into insoluble antinomies and empty dialectic art. For: If thinking is observable, this must mean that it takes its departure not from sense-perceptible data but from its own data; but since data have been declared to be *always and only* sense-perceptible data, this would mean that if thinking were to observe something, then it must itself have created the object it observes.

That an objection of this kind can only be asserted on the basis of a resolute *'that is all'* is obvious to anyone who has dared—even if only once—to rely on the principle of *evidence*. Let us therefore make *evidence* our starting point in order to protect ourselves against not only ordinary but also professional mortals (i.e. our philosophical colleagues). Listen to a philosopher of antiquity, Plotinus: 'All this order of things you must set aside and refuse to see: you must close the eyes and call instead upon another vision which is to be waked within you, a vision, the birthright of all, which few turn to use.'* So: From the standpoint of sane and consistent evidence what does this otherwise *adventurous* sentence mean? If we open our eyes and look at the world around us we of course perceive objects with our senses and then think them on the basis of our perceptions. This is more or less *universally acceptable*. The only question is whether that's all there is to it; in other words, whether our physical eyes can actually see everything there is around us. Even the most elementary (as in Andersen) reflection must lead to a reply in the negative: we only have to concentrate on some object for a moment to realize (quite within the

---

*Plotinus, *The Enneads*, tr. S. MacKenna, (London, Faber & Faber, mcmlxii).

bounds of ordinary common sense) that we are also surrounded by things that are invisible. Looking at a plant we see its external shape and colour, we can touch it and smell it; all this belongs to its external, visible manifestation. But a moment's reflection will lead to the question: Is this visible thing in front of our eyes the whole plant? The plant produces a flower, so we have to deduce that it contains powers of growth that belong to it *objectively* yet are invisible to our physical sight. Should we deny their existence merely because we can't see them? They *exist* independently of 'us', way beyond our sense perceptions. We *think* them, we think them *supersensibly*, in keeping with the way they are, and yet our thinking does not end up in illusions or 'adventures', even though it lacks any sense-perceptible support. The *object* of our thinking is thus brought into being by our thinking, and now this object turns out to be a supersensible reality. We close our eyes and no longer need physical sight, which would be superfluous in this situation. But how do we bring about the transition to this new vision, 'the birthright of all, which few turn to use'? It happened in the instant when our thoughts became absorbed in the *invisible*, when the invisible appeared in all its evidence even though (or rather because) our physical eyes were closed. Who can forbid us to regard this supersensible happening as something we *experience*, something not a jot less reliable than the epoch-making observation of a falling apple or a rolling billiard ball?

Very well (might be the rejoinder of our cleverest colleagues): Perhaps thinking *can* create its own supersensible visions; but this doesn't prove anything except the activity of thinking which constructs reality out of the *a priori* state of its autonomy while knowing no other reality but this one consisting of purely symbolical thought constructs. So what! Here comes the spectre of old Kant, this time in the shrewd *neo-Kantian* shape of his Marburg step-sons (H. Cohen, P. Natorp, and especially E. Cassirer's *Philosophy of*

*Symbolic Forms*). Even in this new disguise the old illusion remains in force: the creative activity of thinking proves to be *conventional* and merely *formal*, and we are not permitted to ask after the real content of these constructs.

The sphere of influence described is based on the unrefuted assumption of a *relativity of subject and object* in which the object is seen as purely physical (regardless of whether it is sense-perceptible as with Kant, or supersensible as with the Marburg School) while the subject is the active element that impresses its *relative* symbols on the world. This sublimated perversion of thinking, having ended up once again in a cul-de-sac, only falls to the ground when faced with the afore-mentioned assumption. After all, we must take into account that the opposition of subject and object is only valid in the physical, sense-perceptible world. I take it into consideration only in so far as I am forced to do so by physical necessity. But if I transpose it into the epistemological realm I make the most blatant mistake of transposition *ab exterioribus ad interiora* (from the outside to the inside) by considering the processes of thinking as being analogous to physical experience. In actual fact, however, a fundamentally different dimension comes into play here that simply will not permit the ordinary relativity of subject and object. Let's try again to come to grips with the fact that thinking is never *situated* in the head although (in the popular view) it does have a very close relationship with the head. Thinking isn't a thing at all that can be 'situated' anywhere. Certainly it is subjective in so far as it comes about through the subject, but at the same time it is *always objective*, because it has no originator *apart from the universe*.

Think *this* thought through, and you will have to admit that your conscious activity of thinking, indeed your conscious mind, i.e. you yourself, are not some kind of monstrous magnetic field pulling any kind of thing into your head, such as a tree, an armchair, a corkscrew, Cleopatra's nose, the stone in Cromwell's bladder, the scrap-iron monument in front of the theatre in Basle or, in the end, the stupidity of your conversation partner. That would be literally to *lose your head*. Not to lose your head means regularly to find yourself *outside* it, i.e. *in* the things (if such prepositions still have any meaning here).

Here is a neat little *evidence* for those who enjoy paradoxes: To be outside oneself means to be in oneself (to preserve one's presence of mind), but to be in oneself means to be outside oneself (to lose one's head). Indeed: Neither does the thing *enter into* thinking only to *emerge again* in the form of a learned expression, nor does thinking *enter into* the thing only to *remain* there in the form of some unspeakable mysticality. Instead *the thought about the thing is the thing itself* (without either 'input' or 'output'). Stop!— cries the bodily, skin-enwrapped representative of our naturalistic habits which is about to burst with rage at what it has heard, and thus jump out of its skin. How can you say such a thing?! Surely the thing is over *there* and the thought *here*: tap tap! The only possible answer to this is: The thing may very well be over *there*, but if we have heard a tapping sound *here* it must have come from knocking on the empty husk of a word rather than on any thought.

The question of *intuitive thinking* thus comes back not to the catalogue of relevant philosophical literature but solely and entirely to *experience*. My 'colleagues', hard of hearing though you may be, please note: not to the concept of experience but to experience itself. In the final analysis all the misfortunes of philosophy can be traced back to this one algorism: *the substitution of the term for thinking*. The term doesn't obscure the thought itself but merely a habit of thought. Consideration of so ordinary an opposition as *rationalism* and *empiricism* will lead to an understanding of the matter in its essentials. The sleight of hand implied in this opposition consists, as we already know, in the assertion that the thought is rational while the sense perception is empirical. In consequence, by falling into the domain of empiricism, our experience becomes merely sense experience, while the thought, having become equated with the concept, is determined out of the region of the non-experiential or super-experiential.

The outcome of this philosophical game of Patience is dreadful, for it is here that a veto is put on intuitive thinking. The judgement remains valid, so it seems. But what is to prevent those of us who are concerned with philosophy (not because we happen to have studied it—and are consequently free to lay it aside at any moment—but because we are so passionately jealous on its behalf) from appealing against the judgement? The situation that prevents us is insultingly obvious and, like all insultingly obvious things, has been consigned to oblivion: Every philosophical proposition exists not for itself but for our mind (always assuming the latter has not yet been turned into a transcendental computer pre-programmed with nothing but philosophical expertise). It follows that every *philosophically sound* assertion can only be tested by an individual mind. Investigation shows, however: Far from being confirmed by personal experience, a *generally valid* philosophical truth usually contradicts such experience and indeed annuls it. Try thinking of something and endeavour to make your thought process as such conform to the above-mentioned opposition of *rationalism-empiricism*. You will soon come to the conclusion that the so-called 'thought' is nothing other than an automatic reaction of a philosophical habit to a given matter. The concrete experience of the matter proves not to be inherent in the act of thinking as such which brings the conceptual form into the material from the outside.

For example: I conceive of a falling stone. The generally valid thought pattern goes like this: The falling stone exists and is shown to me by sense perception, and the corresponding category of understanding exists, which adds the thought of the law of gravity to my perception of the falling stone. This latter is an a priori given added to my thought and logically *precedes* the falling stone so that—speaking with exactitude and *philosophically*—I don't conceive of the falling stone because it is falling, but the stone itself only falls because I conceive of the falling stone. Put in general terms: I don't think like this because this is how it is, but it is like this because this is how I think it is. (*Note from one of his fans*: This is the point at which Monsieur Molière's heroes begin to box ears resoundingly.)

To sum up: The world becomes entirely dependent on the condition of my thinking, whereby I myself am not in the least concerned as to who has made my thinking the way it is. This signifies: Everything that happens in the world—from the viewpoint of its scientific knowability—can only be brought about *like this*; anything that does not come about *like this* but *differently* automatically becomes an illusion or a chimera or—last but not least—poetic licence (assuming that the poetic thought is *different* from the scientific thought which is *like this*).

Let us now permit ourselves to return once more to intuition: What role would be reserved for it in this 'Ministry of Knowledge'? Simply and helplessly we have to say: Its role is unfathomable. It appears to be no more than a werewolf of cognition coming from an assumed 'being different' and pushing its way into 'being like this'; stuffing up our scientifically valid brave new world with all kinds of insights that are free-as-a-bird. Imagine in all seriousness a clock ticking away in its accustomed fashion before all of a sudden—oh! wonder of wonders—going mad at midnight and chiming Augustine's immortal plaintive question: 'What, then, is time? If no one asks of me, I know; if I wish to explain to him who asks, I know not.'\* We could talk of intuition's gauntlet of challenge with the help of which thinking overcomes its profound namelessness and begins

---

\* St Augustine, *Confessions*, XI, 14.

to recall that it is not a clock at all but the clockmaker himself.

The falling stone goes on falling, but now it does not fall because I conceive of it *like this*. Instead, my thinking itself overcomes its own condition (that has been forced upon it) and proves to be merely inherent in the fact of the falling of the stone, so that I, in thinking the fact, think the thought itself, which is given to me inductively in the fact, as its *idea, its law*, indeed *its creative power*, which only in me can express itself as a concept.

This, then, is the *intuitive thought*. By equating it with the bare concept we shut it up inside the head and then struggle in vain with epistemological chatter about subject-object relativity. Intuitive thinking is the eye of the needle through which cognition can survey the immeasurable landscapes of *spiritual science*. Here the thought doesn't appear as a concept but as the *essence of the thing itself*, which is merely mirrored in the concept, and only through this receives its meaning and *reality*. By reducing thinking to bare logic we alienate it from the world, after which we then struggle in vain to reconnect it with the world. Agnosticism is a direct consequence of any train of thought that is interpreted purely discursively. Yet in its original state the thought is synonymous with the world; and the task of cognition is to lift it out of its incognito situation and allow it find its way back to itself in the *cogito*. Only in this manner can I explain to myself Steiner's slogan 'in keeping with reality' which, in the final analysis, proves to be the one and only *norm for cognition*.

Thinking as an *organ of perception*—making an analogy with colour perceived by the eye and sound perceived by the ear, we say:* If colour and sound are *objects* of perception for eye and ear, then thinking also has *objects* of

---

*Or, more correctly, we repeat after Steiner. See R. Steiner, *Goethe the Scientist*, op. cit.

perception which are no less real, indeed with sufficient experience are *more real*, than colour and sound, and these objects of perception of thinking are *ideas*. Let us repeat it again and again: They are ideas neither interpreted from some 'holy writ' nor emanating from some authoritarian mouth, so they are not idols that bungle lives and destinies; they are solely ideas that have been INDIVIDUALLY seen, heard, experienced and transformed into ideals for the orientation and guidance of one's life.

Admirers of the young *philosopher* Steiner later turned away in distaste from Steiner *the scientist of the spirit*. Theosophical admirers of Steiner closed their eyes to Steiner the *methodologist* and *epistemologist*. The former found it impossible that a man whose style was so strictly scientific should suddenly embark on lecturing about the Akashic Record or the mysteries of life after death; the latter couldn't in the least comprehend how the 'greatest occult teacher' could have been an admirer of Ernst Haeckel and Friedrich Nietzsche in his younger years. Between these two extremes of narrow-mindedness—an Achilles lagging behind a tortoise, and a tortoise believing firmly that it cannot be overtaken—lay only one *single, unread book* ...

*A later insertion, not entirely necessary for readers who disagree with what they have read so far*:

The theme here discussed could be reduced to a single key phrase which has, throughout the history of philosophy (especially that of more recent times) almost always proved unlucky. We have mentioned it once already: 'Thinking right through to the end'. 'What has caused me the greatest vexation?' Nietzsche once asked before giving the answer: 'Seeing that no one has the courage any longer to *think things through to the end*.'

Perhaps some future diagnostician of our time will conceive the idea of searching for the root cause of the era's troubles not among all that rubbish about world conspiracy theories but purely and simply in the *dearth of mental and spiritual radicalness*. We do indeed suffer today from a dearth of spiritual radicalness and perhaps for that very reason also from a surfeit of un-spiritual radicalness. What is not taken through to the end in thinking is immediately displaced outwards, whereupon it appears on the scene in all kinds of political or social excesses. The history of the twentieth century is sure to be rewritten one day under a heading that will describe its fundamental mood: 'Cowardly, comfort-seeking thinking—crazy, depraved action.' It is crazy and depraved because it has been deserted by thinking and left to itself in its un-thought-through state.

Let one example stand here for many: What can be more comfort-seeking and cowardly than today's fashion among philosophical journalists to make Nietzsche out to be the godfather of Hitler, setting him up, with journalistic tastelessness, in the dock at Nuremberg—the same Nietzsche who, not afraid to think things through to the end, had prophesied the coming evil more forcefully than any ('You higher men, I will speak clearly and in plain German to you. It is not for *you* that I have been waiting in these mountains'). Let us hope that the *real* godfathers of Hitler (and all the Legion of this century) will one day be unmasked and called by name. It is clear, is it not, to whom I here refer: those honoured academic 'pillars of culture' and that literary riff-raff playing at being hyper-intelligent big-wigs. Perhaps it will gradually come to be more fully realized that nowadays the demons feel at home in places where there is no trace of freedom in thinking. The 'Final Solution'—what a magical formula that can only attain validity in *thinking* and through thinking, for only in thinking can and must *every* problem be finally and, for the world, meaningfully solved. Consider how it became possible for all that was neglected in thinking to fall into the remit of politicians and financiers. One day, too, the history of the atomic bomb will be told in adequate fashion, and not in the manner made popular today by the well-trained stirrup-holders of science; the history of a shameful stain on the tall brow of science that turned aside in arrogance from the culture of the spirit because it was deemed more advantageous to bow and scrape respectfully (and well salaried) before the 'generals'...

Meanwhile, only from present-day occultism in its anthroposophical form can the demand be heard: *Dare to think things through to the end.* This is where the borderline can be drawn between it and all its eastern and western *doppelgängers.* By failing to realize this we find ourselves almost automatically caught in a trap that forces us to choose, like Buridan's ass, between Steiner, the author of *The Philosophy of Freedom*, and Steiner, the author of *Theosophy*. The indivisible, single author of both these books, however, says: 'The trains of thought taken in these two books, though different, lead to the same goal.'* This means that the 'thinking through to the end' of *The Philosophy of Freedom* (or indeed of the whole of Goetheanism) leads inevitably to *Theosophy* or rather *Anthroposophy*. Occultism turns out to be the lot of *every* thought that has the courage to be thought through to the end.

What is meant by thinking through to the end? You can find the answer by trying to do it. When the French naturalist and writer of the eighteenth century, Bernardin de Saint-Pierre, decided to describe a single strawberry leaf *exhaustively*, i.e. *to the end*, he gave up quite soon for the

---

*Preface to the third edition of *Theosophy* (GA 9), tr. M. Cotterell, A.P. Shepherd (London, Rudolf Steiner Press, 1970). Those wishing to find fault with this quotation should feel free to clutch at the lifebuoy of the subsequent sentence: 'For the understanding of the one, the other is by no means necessary, although undoubtedly helpful to some persons.' Yes, indeed. Yet it is precisely with an eye to these 'some' that the creator of anthroposophy has built his whole creation.

tremendous reason that had he persevered it would have fallen to him to describe the whole universe. This is a highly significant example. Once you begin to think anything through *exhaustively* you soon find yourself transported to a range of meaning as wide as the universe. This means: *The principle of the epistemological extent of any thing encompasses the world as a whole.* And please note: We are dealing with the *epistemological,* not the *emotional* extent. The latter can only be justified once it has been taken hold of and secured by thinking. Otherwise the ancient judgement would come into force: 'Fear, and the pit, and the snare, are upon thee, O inhabitant of the earth' (Isaiah, 24,17). The danger of merely *feeling* things through to the end ('There are words in me,' said Nietzsche, 'that would tear the heart of a god to shreds') is for this reason taken in hand and neutralized by *thinking* things through to the end. Armed with the Goethean mine detector, *The Philosophy of Freedom* picks its way through a densely strewn minefield—where Nietzsche the Samurai has set up an apocalyptic display of pyrotechnics. Thinking and feeling anthroposophically always means following things through to the end—without coming to a sad end oneself. As a consequence of following things through to the end one meets with a sad end only if one relies on one's astuteness of feeling while having no faith in one's thinking; this is when one lights upon truths that cannot be contained in the merely psychological realm and therefore tear the soul to shreds.

From hundreds of examples let me chose one at random: 'If you give a penny to a beggar,' said Léon Bloy, 'but do so with a reluctant heart, this penny will sear through the hand of the beggar, will fall to the ground and sear through the earth, will burn a hole in the solar system, traverse the firmament and compromise the universe.' This thoroughly *accurate* vision requires strict *meditative* restraint if it is not to plunge us into despair (*Le Désespéré* is the title of the work by Bloy from which this passage is taken). The incalculable prospects of Socratic 'midwifery' here become apparent, a craft that *universalizes* the tiniest action and thus *normalizes* things that are upside down in ordinary consciousness. For example, an ocean believed to be made up of drops becomes a monstrous thing. This belief is only put back into proportion by thinking: It is not the drop that is *situated in* the ocean—though to many a drip this may seem to be the case—but the ocean that is contained in the drop. If this were not the case the ocean would have to be seen as the sum of the drops, which it would have to be possible to *draw off* and *pour back again*. But what would a drop drawn off be able to make of the ocean? It is a possibility only in the ocean and cannot in any way be imagined as being separate from the whole. Thus does Angelus Silesius marvel from the ground of his being:

Into this little drop, this I, how can it be
That there should flow the whole Sea of the Deity?

This is a revelation for which the ontological possibilities were only created by the *Christ-Event* when the human being Jesus became God by taking into Himself the whole Logos-Ocean of the world. It would be instructive to transpose this principle into the dimension of anthroposophical creativity. If we did, we should have to say that every line by Rudolf Steiner contains within it the whole of the 354-volume collected works (including the thousand times greater sum of all his *silences*).

So now, perhaps as an example of an anthroposophical thinking-through-to-the-end, I find myself considering the impossible, yet unavoidable, statement: An anthroposophist (*per definitionem*) is one who succeeds: firstly, in passing the exam on the subject of *The Philosophy of Freedom* and *Theosophy*; secondly, in taking the foundation seminar in *Knowledge of the Higher Worlds*; thirdly, in getting to know the work of Rudolf Steiner (in part or all of it); fourthly, in thoroughly forgetting all this again; and fifthly—*five*, the *number of freedom*, that's quite something—in beginning to work along anthroposophical lines. No offence meant! But might I not also be entitled to have a go with our by now notorious *'That's all'*?

# 4. 'The thunderous jubilant cry of the Seraphim'

Remarkably, the marginal comments with which Eduard von Hartmann liberally sprinkled the copy of *The Philosophy of Freedom* sent to him by Steiner begin on the title page. It would have been advisable, von Hartmann mused, to call this work 'Epistemological Monism and Ethical Individualism'. Such a rendering of the title undoubtedly mirrors exactly the division of the book into its two parts, but equally undoubtedly such literal reiteration entirely disregards its higher, and indeed sole, purpose. Von Hartmann justified his objections with the remark that a discussion of freedom 'is lacking in the greater part of the book'. Given that from a particular point of view the book deals with the themes covered in all three of Kant's critiques (in the first part the *epistemological* theme of *Critique of Pure Reason*, in the second the *moral* theme of *Critique of Practical Reason*, and, encompassing the two, the *freedom* theme of *Critique of Teleological Judgment*), von Hartmann's dissection of the *synthetic* aspect into two *analytical* constituents, cognition and morality, appears to be almost purposeful.

This would indeed leave no room for a discussion of freedom in the traditional sense. Freedom discussed in the ordinary manner doesn't combine with epistemology, which is subject to *logical* necessity, nor with morality, which is subject to *ethical* necessity, so that the remaining domain would be limited either to *metaphysical* tracts or purely theological problems, or—in the last, worst instance—to a merely *aesthetic* backyard in the sense of Pope Paul III's rather dubious interpretation of the formula in connection with Benvenuto Cellini's excesses: 'One must take account of the fact that individuals like Benvenuto, who are unique in their artistic ability, cannot be subject to any laws.'

Von Hartmann's reaction to the title of the book and then to its content was entirely traditional. The utter novelty, the complete newness of the work simply escaped him. The domain of freedom in *The Philosophy of Freedom* occupies the central position both in the realm of *cognition* and in that of *morality*, uniting the two with an artistic flair that is 'not subject to any law'. Steiner described the transition from the first to the second part of the book as 'the power that leads from scientific ideas—which are ethically neutral—into the sphere of moral impulses'.* If anything at all were to contradict the traditional attitudes of modern times it would have to be a transition of this kind. By the end of the nineteenth century, knowledge and morality had become so divergent and mutually opposed that only the most cunning bigotry and hypocrisy might perhaps have been capable of making them conform with one another in practice. As in the classic tale of one hand busily building up what the other kept pulling down in a drunken frenzy, science, ethically neutral, was *mechanically* complemented by a cognitively neutral morality. Descartes was quite capable of atheistic raging in his scientific constructions while at the same time embarking on a pilgrimage to Our Lady of San Loreto. Newton had no difficulty in emptying the cosmos of deities while retaining the habit of baring his head at every mention of the name of God.

The good Count Laplace proved a great deal more frank and plucky with the *'ecco e basta'* he ventured in reply to Napoleon's enquiry as to God, for whom there appeared to be no place in his cosmogony: 'Your Majesty, I had no need for that hypothesis.' Much less brave was his cosmogonical accomplice, ever the same old crafty Kant, who used science

---

*R. Steiner, *An Autobiography* (GA 28), tr. R. Stebbing (Blauvelt, Steinerbooks, 1977, p. 257).

to drive out the spectre of the immortal soul by unmasking it as humbug while at the same time forcing people morally to believe in the humbug!

In short: Cognition without morality was transformed into purely scientific 'Sodom', while morality without cognition became merely the heel-clicking habit of 'Yes, sir!'. Let us raise all those patron demons of the risible and ask ourselves in all seriousness: What could be more pathological than those typically modern scenes in which worthy Nobel laureates first fulfil their 'contract' to abolish our planet and then rush in a bellowing crowd to sign those pathetic declarations about the 'moral responsibility of the scientist'! Let us be honest and admit: If cognition without morality amounts to Holbach's *'Système de la nature'*, then the resulting moral eructation has to be a Marquis de Sade who, by the way, declared himself quite openly to be a follower of 'Holbachism'.*

Thus did morality, lacking any cognitive foundation, degenerate. Obviously, though, moral degeneration had to be preceded by cognitive decline: an ethically neutral science which—lacking any input of inherently moral impulses—could not help sliding down into technical wizardry and engineering ingenuity, only to end up ruefully banging the moral warning gong without being able to exert any influence. It has to be understood that morality can only survive on the basis of cognition. By giving cognition a miss and making straight for morality, freedom could not help becoming freedom *from* morals. So the alarming alternative came to be an amoral freedom or an unfree morality.

The death blow administered to the latter by Friedrich Nietzsche opened the door to *total nihilism*. Only remember

---

*'Holbach's system constitutes the real and indisputable foundation of my philosophy; I would follow him blindly, if necessary *even into martyrdom*' [Sade's emphasis]. Sade, *Lettres choisies* (Paris, 1963, p. 143).

the icy prognosis uttered by him, the man who once termed himself the *freest human being in Europe*:* 'What I am telling you is the story of the next two centuries. I am describing what is coming, what can no longer be prevented: the *rise of nihilism*.'† And here is another explosion of that paroxysm becoming aware of itself: 'I know my fate. One day there will be associated with my name the recollection of something frightful—of a crisis like no other before on earth, of the profoundest conflict of conscience, of a decision evoked *against* everything that until then had been believed in, demanded, sanctified.'‡ The profoundest conflict of conscience: having to choose between honest nihilism and dishonest morality, and to give preference to nihilism because in the deepest depths of your soul you remain the most moral among men (Nietzsche—*the little saint*, '*il piccolo santo*' as seen by a chance travelling companion who did not know his books).

The 'sadistic' conclusions offered by this choice, that pricked Sade on to *practise* depravity and crime, were by Nietzsche turned in upon himself. The goad of uncontrollable freedom finally drove him into madness. This Nietzschean madness is now transformed by Steiner into a soundness of soul such as has never before existed; yet Nietzsche's madness proved to be more than the personal fate of the 'godless one, the pied piper of consciences'. It became the potential destiny of an age that lost its questionable Victorian soundness once and for all in Nietzsche.

Thus we arrive at the pinnacle of contemporary idiocy: The author of *The Philosophy of Freedom* came to be regarded

---

*In the letter to Overbeck dated 30 April 1884. Friedrich Nietzsche, *Sämtliche Briefe*, ed. Colli and Montinari (Munich, 1986, Vol. 6, p. 189).
† Friedrich Nietzsche, *Nachgelassene Fragmente 1887–1889*. Critical edition, Vol. 13, p. 189.
‡ Friedrich Nietzsche, *Ecce Homo*, tr. R.J. Hollingdale (London, Penguin Classics, 1979).

as a Nietzschean. Ferdinand Tönnies, professor in Kiel (one of the future 'Cerberuses' of German sociology), even developed this nonsense in quite a churlish manner. But such silliness can be forgiven so long as it is nothing more than another example of professional imbecility! The fact, however, that this book by Steiner was closely bound up with Nietzsche, and that Nietzsche's profoundest conflict of conscience here met its solution—this is one of the unique events in recent cultural history.

Here, for the first time, was a demonstration of *how to philosophize with a hammer* without the philosopher smashing up his own sanity. In the letter to Rosa Mayreder quoted earlier this is clearly stated: 'I have to confess that it pains me to know that Nietzsche was no longer capable of reading my book. He would have taken it for what it is: in every line a *personal* experience.' And even more forcefully in a letter to Pauline Specht written at about the same time: 'Nietzsche's illness pains me greatly. For I am convinced that my "freedom philosophy" would not have passed him by unnoticed. He would have found that I have taken further a quantity of questions he left unanswered; and I'm sure he would have agreed that his view of morality, *his immoralism, finds its culmination in my "freedom philosophy"* [emphasis by K.S.], that his "moral instincts", properly sublimated and followed to their roots, amount to what I call "moral imagination". The chapter on "Moral Imagination" in my "freedom philosophy" is entirely lacking in Nietzsche's *Genealogy of Morals* even though everything in this points in that direction. And his *Anti-Christ* is merely a particularized confirmation of my own view.'*

By the way, and in order to have done with any kind of imbecility: It is not of Steiner's 'Nietzscheanism' we should be speaking but, if we must, rather of Nietzsche's 'Steinerism', for although he failed to achieve his *own* 'freedom

---

*R. Steiner, *Briefe II*, op. cit.

philosophy', he sacrificed everything to make the writing of Steiner's book possible. The whole force of Nietzsche's longing, the tearing urge to find *unconditional and uninhibited morality* that tortured him like an inflamed nerve every time he touched on moral values ('I had to abolish morality', he confessed, 'in order to enforce my moral will'), has found astonishing and crystal clear correspondences in *The Philosophy of Freedom*.

For Nietzsche himself it became the black hole of insanity. *Unconditional morality*, not made legitimate by *unconditional cognition*, merely bared its teeth in the grimace of nihilism and cynicism. For what else is *nihilism* (assuming it has fermented in the light of cognition and not in Heidegger's Black Forest brewery) but *unconditionality* that has slipped from the realm of thinking into the zone of feeling and will, thus losing the capacity to *function through cognition* and becoming instead destructive passion? Nietzsche's whole tragedy is in the end the tragedy of a gnostic led astray by philology who set too much store by style and imagined he could fence against the hellish 'armoured divisions' of subtlest lies with an aphoristic dagger. Paul's rule, 'The pneumatic can judge all things, yet he himself is judged by no one' (I Cor. 2,15), has turned into a paradox: In this instance the one who 'judges all things' was not one gifted with *spirit* (a *pneumatic*, a *gnostic*) but merely with *soul* (a *psychic*); he therefore did not judge but was judged, and soon any barrack-room boy was allowed to write commentaries on him. No wonder he was only a stone's throw away from the nearest psychiatrist!

Meanwhile, however, the matter in hand was, in fact, *gnosis* of the purest sort, gigantic *spiritual* tasks that had been drowned in the sound and fury of a 'soulfulness' gone crazy. Soulfulness devoid of spirit leads directly to a relish for high-flown wind-baggery, to the tastelessness of the shilling shocker, to the narrow-minded clipped syllables of the sergeant-major. *Unconditionality* thus appeared on the scene, having avoided epistemology and squandered itself on a *'gaya scienza'* instead.

Nietzsche's announcement 'God is dead', an intentionally theatrical formulation, contains neither an encodement of the West's threadbare metaphysics (as some would have it) nor the shallow pathology of a religious atheism (as others have tried to prove) but yet again the same demand for unconditionality. It is an unconditionality that makes Nietzsche 'the deicide' appear related not so much to all kinds of 'Byronically melancholy demons' as to Meister Eckhart, who formulated Nietzsche's thesis in astonishing words not a jot less radical: 'May it please God to make me quits with God.'* Eckhart, though, was a *master* in that his words were not presented as a dainty morsel the *aroma* of which drew the market flies of every land to fancy themselves as the 'driving force of history'. Nietzsche's formulation, on the other hand, has worked like an aromatic dainty morsel of this kind for over a century.

When Steiner stated in the foreword of his book on Nietzsche† that he had arrived, independently and along different routes, at views that harmonize with those of Nietzsche, we must see the 'harmony' as referring in the first place to the *unconditionality*, and the 'different routes' to *cognition*, together with the epistemological treatment of the freedom question. For none may enjoy the *reality of freedom* without having first undergone the difficult schooling of the *science of freedom*. The path to morality can only lead via cognition; and freedom that does not take its start from the freeing of thinking, but slips instead straight into the zone of the instincts, is nothing but a terrible *doppelgänger* of freedom, infecting us with a *mania for freedom* and declaring

---

*Meister Eckhart, *Predigten und Schriften* (Frankfurt/Hamburg 1956, p. 195).
† R. Steiner, *Friedrich Nietzsche. Fighter for Freedom* (GA 5), tr. M. Ingram (New Jersey, Rudolf Steiner Publishers, 1960).

as free every 'I will', whether it be *I will* smash glasses, or *I will* grunt. An image of freedom such as this is the opposite, indeed a caricature, of the Gospel story about the man of Gadara possessed with unclean spirits: it is not the unclean spirits being driven into the swine but the swinish spirit making the unclean ones even worse.

The only legitimate 'I will' that can lead us to genuine freedom at this stage is: 'I will know'. With this there can begin within us the practical freeing of thinking from the terminological usurpers clinging to it (and indeed their name is Legion). Once thinking has become free, and recognized itself as the creative power of the universe, it begins to regard itself as *obligation* and *responsibility* towards the world. We say of individuals that they are free if they act in accordance with their nature and are not checked by any outward constraint. This undeniable truth at once becomes shrouded in countless misunderstandings and silly talk if it is founded not on thinking that is pure and free but on feelings and instincts and murky urges of the will. Multitudes of swindlers immediately appear—from those who only yesterday were still their mothers' darlings and on to the most hardened adventurers—each and every one laying a claim to this truth and declaring high and low: We, too, are acting in accordance with our nature, which is thus and thus, and so we, too, are free! But this 'free-for-all' freedom has no trace of freedom in it—only the insolence of those who have got out and done a bunk from the moral cage in order to roll in the muck of amoral urges. For to live in accordance with one's own nature one must *know* this nature, not in the lowest and most egoistical disguise of moody selfishness but in its original *innateness*.

What would happen to the world if umpteen millions of such wilful natures were to come up against one another all for the sake of their 'free-for-all' freedom? Hobbes's 'war of all against all' which amounts, in the end, to having Sodom and Gomorrah as the capital city of the New World Order.

(Tough luck, my fellow citizens of today!) To know my own nature means to stop indulging its whims; it means to know it through and through to the point where it receives no stimulus from outside but is left entirely to itself; it means to know it to the point where I discover its power of thinking that reveals the content of the universe and confronts me with a shattering choice: If you want to remain an egoist, then do so! But henceforth your egoism must assert itself *in the whole cosmos*, for your ego itself, which hitherto you thought to be your private property, is by no means there to serve the satisfaction of your personal whims; it belongs to world events at large. Take note: What you are being told is no Sunday sermon, no Salvation Army pamphlet; it is 'Results of introspective observation following the methods of natural science', and therefore no less strict and exact than those you can find in textbooks of physics and mathematics. This, then, is the *nature of thinking*, that *ens reale* and *absolutum* that all metaphysicians thought they had found in the beyond but which now turns out to be attainable solely through *thinking as the eye of the needle*—neither in the here and now nor in the beyond, but in thinking itself.

For: When I think, I am not only observing the evolution of the world but participating in it *actively*. Thinking opens the door through which I can not only enter the *workshop* of the heavenly hierarchies but also leave again and return to the world. My attitude is then no longer that of an observer in mind but of a *participant* (here The Philosophy of Freedom merely represents the foundation course in *theological matters*) who, despite being loaded with all the weight of world responsibility, can carry it with the buoyant and airy gait of a eurythmist. 'For my yoke is easy, and my burden is light'—words spoken by the Redeemer, the wondrous meaning of which is only revealed in such moments of knowledge. It is more than obvious that *this* thinking is not only thinking but also *will*, where now every 'I will' no longer lives in the eternal treadmill of moods and whims but in accordance with its own *divine* nature, which was once *revelation* but is now *experience*.

Here a new, reborn *morality* steps forth: the practice of moral imagination, perhaps the rarest of all the pearls scattered throughout *The Philosophy of Freedom*. Such pages are written once in every thousand years, and though at first there may be no resonance on earth, their echo resounds across the heavens in a flash as the *'thunderous jubilant cry of the Seraphim'* (to use Dostoevsky's beautiful words). I don't know what was happening on earth while this book was being written, but I do know that the firmament leaned down towards the spot where it was coming into being, drawing closer to it than to any other place on the globe.

Let us consider what it was that occurred—but first we had better call to mind what was there before. Morality was there before; you could conform to it or not, you could keep it or disregard it, you could get worked up about it or duck out of it. But no eminent or lively or in any way exceptional individual could have succeeded *in suppressing a yawn* about it. What devilish exclusivity must have been needed to give such lofty truths so disgustingly boring and insipid an appearance—to the approval of all those 'maiden aunts' of the world and the amusement of all their 'naughty nephews'! Morality as a military barracks, morality as a circus trainer, morality as scarecrow even, these might have been bearable—just about—provided there was still a chance to rebel, to throw down a gauntlet, obstinately to refuse. But morality as a yawn, morality as a soporific, morality as the chastity of a well-read and frigid female fan of Rousseau—the only thing left in the face of this was a shrug of resignation. Vasili Rozanov, sarcastic as he was, once wrote a note while travelling. 'On Morality' was the heading, followed by 'St Petersburg to Kiev, railway carriage'. It bore frank witness to that resignation: 'I don't even know whether "morality" is spelt with one "l" or two; nor who its papa and mama were, nor whether it had any children; and what is its address—I haven't the faintest idea.'

Understandably, anything even slightly vivacious or original had to escape from this quarantine of anonymity and go in search of infection as though hunting for manna from heaven. Morality, shallow and plain, was challenged by anything *vibrant or pithy*—with all the bizarre and sudden surprises that entailed, be it the simple urge to scandalize or the seismic irruptions of the artistic genius. Its antinomy was most clearly seen by the early writers of the nineteenth century. Their manifesto is Kierkegaard's *Either/Or*, in which pleasure and duty, the unique *aesthetic moment* and tedious *ethical eternity*, collided. Aesthetic abhorrence of morality verges on the pathological and anomalous; the whole menagerie of amorality is mobilized to avoid falling victim to moral sterility: cynicism, arrogance, mendacity, mockery, the romanticizing of evil; and, spilling over directly into lifestyle: alcoholism, narcotics, perversions, even suicide. Flaubert, enthusing about lepers in Jerusalem: 'What a spectacle for colourists like us!' 'If I succeed,' he wrote in a letter, 'in finding rottenness and gangrene where others see only purity and beauty, I lift up my head and laugh.' Baudelaire, manically breeding his *Fleurs du mal* in the face of the perfumed bouquets of bourgeois virtue, sings the praises of 'carrion' in one of the most beautiful poetic works of the century. Oscar Wilde's scandal-tempting phrase spreads a mischievous odour of moral sanctity over the author of elegantly aesthetic essays on the history of art: 'The fact of a man being a poisoner is nothing against his prose.' And roaring down from the seven solitudes of his Engadine retreat comes Nietzsche who is 'criminally radical': 'I see more inclination to greatness in the feelings of Russian nihilists than in those of English utilitarians.' This is the *ultima ratio* of the programme statement of Nietzsche's Theo- or rather Cosmodicy to the effect that: 'the existence of the world is only justified as an aesthetic phenomenon'. At the same time the 'Russian Nietzsche' Konstantin Leontev almost expires in impotent rage against the rise of universal paltriness: 'How terrible, how offensive it is to think that Moses ascended Mount Sinai, that the Hellenes erected such beautiful Acropolises, that the Romans conducted the Punic Wars, that the young genius Alexander crossed the Granicus wearing his feathered helmet and fought before the walls of Arbela, that the Apostles preached, the martyrs suffered, the singers sang, the painters painted and the knights excelled themselves at jousting—only for some French, or German or Russian bourgeois in his ugly and comical garb to live without a care either "collectively" or "individually" upon the ruins of all this bygone greatness.'

If we multiply these examples tenfold we shall perhaps begin to understand what a terrible gulf there was between tedious, plain morality and the soul's unquenchable need for bright and dazzling colours. A question, oppressive as a nightmare: Is it really true that to be virtuous we must at any cost be boring? Or the opposite: Is only evil capable of being vibrant and fascinating?

Morality's reaction was not long in coming: Anything above the ordinary was held to be demonic; vengeance was wrought on those genial deserters with ample application of the weaponsmith's wide range of poisonous and avenging implements. A Norwegian critic appealed in public to have Henrik Ibsen whipped; an English journalist, a third-rate literary scribbler, pushed through the crowd around Oscar Wilde on his way from law court to prison and spat in his face. We can imagine the sigh of relief, audible across Europe, when the learned psychiatrists began to get involved and produced the diagnosis: *Genius is madness.* Thus did morality take its revenge. But none of these acts of vengeance saved it from the diagnosis of its own complaint: *Morality is a yawn.*

The next thing to happen was utterly improbable. *The Philosophy of Freedom* wrought a miracle by wrenching morality from the clutches of rote-learned good behaviour and giving it back to experience: HENCEFORWARD IT WAS POSSIBLE IN MORALS, TOO, FOR GENIUS TO EXIST. What Schiller, amazingly, foresaw in his *Letters on the Aesthetic Education of Man* (morality rescued through play), what l'abbé Galiani once expressed with exceptional aptness,* what Nietzsche almost grasped in his dreams about morality as instinct,† and what drew from Vladimir Soloviev the burning call for 'the inspiration of the good'— through Steiner's book all this became sunlit reality and *possibility.* Hitherto presumed to be the prerogative of art and accorded only grudging recognition by science, imagination now relieved morality of its hackneyed duties and set it free by uniting it with the human ego. An axiom, mathematically irrefutable, came true: *Morality is creative doing—or it is nothing.*

Imagine Oscar Wilde again, that prodigal genius of amorality. What would happen if he began—without in the least ceasing to be catastrophically unique—to put all his genius into moral deeds, laying his bets now not on artistic masterpieces to be finished in a trice but on *masterpieces of moral action*? Dorian Gray, devoted voluntarily to deeds of

---

* In his letter to Madame d'Epinay dated 26 April 1777: 'Morality has only been able to maintain itself among human beings because little was spoken about it, in particular never on any account in a didactic manner, but always eloquently and poetically. If the Jesuits were to conceive the idea of making a system of it, they would mutilate it beyond recognition. Basically, virtue is an enthusiasm.' *Correspondance inédite de l'abbé Galiani* (Paris, 1818, p. 437).

† The hammer speaks: 'One must be exceedingly immoral [i.e.: free, K.S.] to act morally.' Friedrich Nietzsche, *Nachgelassene Fragmente,* op. cit., p. 453.

selfless goodness, would reverse the correlation between the 'sitter' and the 'portrait'. The countenance of the sitter, downcast by defamation, would develop lines of suffering, while the hidden portrait (Bosch's *Kerchief of St Veronica*) would glow day by day with increasing, unbearable beauty. Imagine Byron living a life of virtue with Parnassus in the service of morality; or Baudelaire's *Fleurs du mal* changing into the 'little flowers' of St Francis or the *'blaue Blume'* of Novalis. Imagining these things might lead to a comprehension of the Manichaean significance of what has happened.

Whatever until now has been the pride and attested prerogative of *aristocratic bohemianism*—taste, elegant gestures, the art of speaking through the corner of the mouth, sensational wit, long-suffering cynicism, infrared and ultraviolet frequencies of perception, indeed the whole 'demonic' technique of exceptional individuals and idiosyncratic personalities—all this is transported into the realm of morality that suddenly becomes as stunningly impressive as hitherto only art could be. Morality no longer submits to the call of the categorical imperative but to the inexpressible sighs of its own muse's inspiration, as though it were now a matter not so much of works of art created over years but of ordinary, every-day, momentary masterpieces. I may share my artistic freedom with the capricious genius of inspiration, waiting in trembling anticipation day by day for it to seize me by my forelock, turn me towards the East and say: 'Paint what you see over there!' But my *moral* freedom is shared with no one, which denotes: My moral inspiration does not depend upon chance or the impenetrable caprices of my Dionysian companions but solely upon my very own WILL, now lit by thinking, having come to itself and been filled with spirit.

Moral genius (and therein lies its miraculous incomparability) is neither élitist nor selective, but ever-present everywhere, like the parables in the Gospels, which illuminate the secrets of the cosmos in scenes of every day. It can be practised at any moment, so that its norm is no longer the 'today I'm a genius' of Pushkin and Blok (tragically and helplessly wounded by the defeats of *yesterday* and *tomorrow*, where Pushkin, the genius of *today*, yesterday increased his cunning tricks like Don Giovanni only to gain tomorrow the lot of an 'unlucky devil' and be slain by anyone happening to pass his way) but a never-ending state of continuous geniality. There is no 'yesterday' *or* 'today' raised to dizzying heights above the 'every-day', but only the 'always' ever-present in the 'midst of the every-day scene'.

This morality, utterly extraordinary and never seen until now, is *the one and only normal* morality. For we might as well admit: Although the democratic psychiatrists succeeded in equating genius with abnormality, the last word in the matter of this diagnosis was reserved not for scientific open-mindedness but for *the predominant majority of the opposite camp.* Where the norm was decreed by the *grey* majority, the *startling* minority automatically transposed itself into the realm of pathology. In actual fact the normality of morality signified majority.* From here its feelers reached right into the region of cognition in which, as the *doppelgänger* of moral generality, *logical* generality occurred. Only what remained *individual* in scope and exclusivity continued to be an exception by scraping a miserable and semi-legal existence in *aesthetic* exile stripped of any moral or cognitive rights.

---

*What this latter signified and will always signify can be found expressed by Goethe in a formulation of mathematical precision: 'Nothing is more repulsive than the majority: for it consists of few powerful leaders, of rogues who accommodate themselves, of the weak who are assimilated, and of the masses who follow along behind without in the least knowing what they want.' *Goethes Naturwissenschaftliche Schriften*, Vol. 5 (Dornach, 1982, p. 400).

Alas, the exception proved the rule. Since it seemed impossible to prevent the appearance on the scene of a Rembrandt, a Goethe or a Beethoven,* the only alternative was to confiscate their works. Justice would not have been done to the majority by presuming that they could not cope with the exceptional. Though perhaps they can't cope with it in *ordinary life*, they can ogle it in *exhibitions* and *concert halls* where it is put on show to flatter the low-brows and contribute to their 'aesthetic recreation'. However ninefold the shattering effect of the Ninth Symphony on the cosmos might be, its rights are restricted to the radius of *concerts* or *recordings*, for any disturbance of this radius might provoke a disruption by 'fellow human beings' and all kinds of 'excessive behaviour'.

But now look at the opposite picture. Here the majority is pathological and genius the norm, so 'moral bolshevism' makes way for the 'ethical individualism' of *The Philosophy of Freedom*. Only then can the Ninth Symphony (no matter where: in concert hall or—dare I say it?—*headphones*) be appreciated no longer merely as an aesthetic masterpiece but also as *normal behaviour*, not as something unique but as an unlimited possibility that cannot in any way be shut up in the isolation of a concert cell unless it should happen that life itself becomes a concert.

Moral imagination, moral genius, is something *Dionysian* that has been transported from art to morality where it no longer breathes the Pythian fumes but the freely contemplating mind. Sporadically yet unstoppably this Dionysian morality pierces through the fabric of our patterns of behaviour. If the right to imagination succeeds in achieving validity in the historical dimension, I believe that the day will come when bewildered historians will

---

* Though in the twentieth century a specialist science, *genetic engineering*, was to be created for this purpose, a 'Nobel'-bait that more than one scholarly fish would attempt to snap up.

want to speak of a *moral renaissance*, a 'quattrocento' and 'cinquecento' of the flowering of *moral* genius. Forging ahead, the *genius of goodness* will become creative with a virtuosity and to an extent that will equal that earlier production of immortal paintings and sculptures wherever you looked in every little Italian town.

We must bring home to ourselves the fact that the trail for this renaissance has already been blazed and that no power anywhere—no 'shadowy brotherhoods'—will be capable of erecting a barrier across it, for morality itself has *joined forces* with its eternal enemy—the *potent, independent, free individual*, so that the latter may be saved from amorality and morality itself from insignificance. This morality acknowledges the most rapacious individualism (like Stirner's, like Nietzsche's) yet it remains true to the letter and the spirit of every commandment ever issued. Yes, indeed! The Sinai tablets of Moses reconstructed by Max Stirner! Is that a paradox? Not at all; it is the interpretation of Christ's words: 'Think not that I am come to destroy the Law, or the Prophets: I am not come to destroy, but to fulfil' (Math. 5,17). That is: The law is henceforth no longer synonymous with an automatic 'Thou shalt' but with the thought-filled, individual 'I will'. Now that this 'I will' has attained its majority in the likes of Max Stirner the next step on its path, rescuing it from the absurdity of unconscious wilfulness, will be the way to the Jordan, or *baptism in thinking*, in which *individual will* unfailingly unites with *universal duty*. Not: 'Love thy neighbour!', but: '*I* love my neighbour', for that is what I *wish*, and I '*can do no other*'.

Morality so excessively individual grows beyond the merely individual and on into the social realm—into *truth, beauty, goodness*. What superhuman strength was needed to bring back to life the startlingly, deeply moving, original meaning of this trinity that has been talked to tatters of banality for centuries! And in such a manner that not a sheep-eyed Abel but that 'poisoner and prose stylist' mentioned earlier would tremble with jubilation at it!* Not even Leo Tolstoy, backed by the mighty authority of being a universal genius, was able to escape the mockery when he reached out spontaneously for 'the book of life'. So what could a young and hardly known 'doctor of philosophy' possibly do when a fire-, water-, and air-proof professor called him a 'Nietzsche fancier', and another (how dare we call him that!) 'colleague' persisted in recommending, after *The Philosophy of Freedom* was published, that he might do well to read Wundt and Benno Erdmann.

---

* Later—in outlining a threefold way of shaping human society—Steiner was to bring back to life the startlingly original meaning of another trinity long since talked to tatters of banality: *Liberty, Equality, Fraternity.*

## 5. 'The most Christian of philosophies'

Finally we come to the brightly shining crux of this deeply absorbing biography of freedom. 'The most Christian of philosophies' is what Rudolf Steiner once called *The Philosophy of Freedom.*\* In this sense, too, the thesis of unconditionality remains in force, giving the book a dimension of *unconditional Christianity*—for surely in any other dimension it would have to be considered anti-Christian. There is no doubt that modern 'scientific' atheism itself is a somewhat wobbly and ambiguous matter, for science, ethically neutral, leaves you free to choose between Satan and the Devil. It would not be hard to collect plenty of examples that bear this out. Finding the way to *Christ*, however, is something it does not permit, for finding Christ would confront it with its own 'Damascus'. Let us not forget that Saul 'yet breathing out threatenings and slaughter against the disciples', also believed in God and was no atheist. He became Paul, and a Christian, only when 'suddenly there shined about him a light from heaven'.

By curing cognition of the lock-jaw of ethical neutrality and reviving it with moral impulses, *The Philosophy of Freedom* now turns out to be a 'Damascus' of this very kind for our present time. Without it you might just as well be a believer as an atheist—and without it, equally, it will be granted to none to become a *Christian*. (Who can tell whether a gauntlet of this kind, thrown down in present-day 'Christian' Europe, will meet with any indignation

---

\* R. Steiner, *The Human Soul in Relation to World Evolution* (GA 212), tr. R. Stebbing (New York, Anthroposophic Press, 1984, lecture of 7 May 1922).

whatsoever, or indeed whether a Christian 'Salman Rushdie'—not merely a counterpart to the real one, but as an incident, a precedent—is still a possibility today?)

Once again I cannot help quoting Nietzsche, for I know of none other who would be willing, with such self-destructive integrity, to conduct autopsies on the rotting preserves offered in the market-place today dressed up in enticingly labelled tins: 'Our age *knows*,' he said, and hence 'it is indecent to be a Christian today. *And here is where my disgust commences.*' 'Where,' he cried, 'have the last feelings of decency and self-respect gone when even our statesmen, in other ways a very unprejudiced kind of man and practical anti-Christians through and through, still call themselves Christians today and go to Communion?' And finally, as Nietzschean as anything: 'What a *monster of falsity* modern man must be that he is nonetheless *not ashamed* to be called a Christian!' Thus speaks that hurricane of a book: *The Anti-Christ*.

Are there any left among us in whom such uncompromising honesty, powerful as a force of nature, has not quite died out and who would still prefer not to stand before God like fools? Let any such cross their heart and ask *whether this is not so, indeed*! And let them also ask whether *such* disgust, *such* fury, whether a feeling of *such* abhorrence is not so much the sign of an *anti-Christian* as of an *early* Christian finding himself set down among impenetrable *pseudo-Christianity*? Nietzsche's fury, breaking all bounds in its final, irresponsible paroxysm of passion, is nothing other than the unrecognized reaction of a *pure* Christian to the 'abominable devastation'. For my part, this is the only explanation I have for the young Steiner's enthusiasm on reading *The Anti-Christ* soon after *The Philosophy of Freedom* was published: 'Nietzsche's *Anti-Christ* ... is one of the most significant books to have been written in centuries. It expresses my own feelings in every sentence. I have so far found no words with which to express the degree of satisfaction this book arouses in me.'*

The question following on from the very nature of Nietzsche's attacks should have been: How is Christianity possible? It is not a matter of searching for a Christian who, as Goethe put it, is 'like Christ would have wanted him to be'. Our question has a more poisonous bite: Can there still be a Christianity today that need not be thought of as

---

* From the letter to Pauline Specht dated 23 December 1894. The fact that thirty years later, during the karma lectures given in 1924, Nietzsche's *Anti-Christ* was described by Steiner as being direct inspiration from Ahriman, does not contradict Steiner's youthful experience in any way, but rather illumines it *esoterically*. However: A number of activists in the anthroposophical movement in the West have long been busy trying to trip Steiner up, with the oh! so noble aim of de-mystifying him and returning him to the fold of the all-too-humanly fickle, though in fact all they want is to draw him down to their own level. (In an essay by, well, an 'anthroposophist' Steiner figures as a 'product of his time', not immune to momentary emotions and nationalistic prejudices.) These people have used such so-called 'contradictions' to conclude that Steiner was an atheist in his young days. An appropriate comment here would surely be: 'Don't get too big for your boots.' This is what happens when intellects trained in philosophical and journalistic kitsch stir about haughtily and arrogantly in esoteric matters whose very nature it is to consist of nothing *but* such 'contradictions'! Incidentally, it is worth noting that Ahriman, who inspired Nietzsche—'a part of that power which always *wills* the bad, and always works the good' (yet another of those extraordinary contradictions!)—has once again ended up doing good by giving the final blow to a Christianity that had been a lie for centuries, thereby preparing the soil for the new, *unconditional* Christianity which later came to feature in Steiner's Christology. Seen in this light, the enthusiasm of the young author of *The Philosophy of Freedom* for Nietzsche's *Anti-Christ* is not unlike the obligation Hercules would have felt towards any other hero, had such a one cleaned out the Augean stables on his behalf. Indeed, I would tend to state this even more strongly: *The Anti-Christ* had to be written, and had Nietzsche not done so, and had a third Hercules been lacking, Steiner would have had to write it himself, which, as things turned out, fortunately proved unnecessary.

merely an indolence of inherited capacities, in other words something *indecent*? Can there be a Christianity that is 'the way, the truth and the life', or that is, in the words of Kierkegaard, 'eternally contemporaneous with Christ'?

We repeat: *Our age knows*. Here we have the stumbling-block and entire dialectic of misunderstandings deriving from it, and also that dialectic of disgust. The various possibilities can be worked out mathematically. To be a Christian in our age would mean: either to know one thing while believing in another, or to know one thing while pretending to believe in the other, or to know nothing while merely believing in the other. Admittedly, the first two variants would hardly pass even the simplest test in Christianity; and the third—Luther's *sola fide*—would only have sufficed for the Christianity of *past times* with all the subsequent improprieties arising from those times that exist today. Nietzsche came to the terrible conclusion that cost him his life: 'It therefore follows that Christianity is impossible.' Here the young Steiner stepped in and called a halt. And most importantly he did so not from outside but *from inside* everything that is to be found in The Anti-Christ, in entire agreement with all preceding preconditions: Christianity is possible as the *fourth variant*. It is not: to know one thing while believing in another, nor to pretend to believe in the other, nor merely to believe in the other. It is: TO KNOW THE OTHER.

This is where *The Philosophy of Freedom* makes its appearance, the *most Christian* of books, pointing the lance of its knowledge at what has hitherto been the domain of faith. Agreeing with Nietzsche, Rudolf Steiner also said: Our age *knows*. But what is this knowledge that it has? This is the question Nietzsche failed to ask and which therefore plunged him into breakdown. Arming himself for a campaign against holy relics of a thousand years ago, Prince Free-as-a-Bird got stuck with a positivism and scepticism too hastily mobilized while setting up his epistemological premises; as though here, too, the madness of Gascony had come in handy as a way of conquering this 'Paris'.

The answer given by *The Philosophy of Freedom* is: Christianity is possible *with knowledge*, but for this you need a Christian epistemology or, as Steiner was to say later about *Truth and Knowledge* as well as about *The Philosophy of Freedom*, 'Pauline thoughts in the realm of the theory of knowledge'. Paul (the 'patron saint of thinking in Christianity', in Albert Schweitzer's beautiful expression), the least understood—or simply 'hard to be understood' as the Apostle Peter put it (II Peter 3,16)—perhaps the most lonely spirit of all who have ever become known in the Christian world; Paul—the patron and advocate of every kind of spiritual rebellion and 'dissidence' that is branded with the hot irons of a desire to know and with the *spirit of freedom*, here unrecognized even by the rebel (Nietzsche) himself; Paul—the Moses of Christianity, leading its living spirit out of the new prison of Rome and Constantinople and indeed out of any other prison as well, wherever that spirit finds itself hampered by the plaster of Paris of the 'nomenclature' or done up in its own death mask; Paul—who like no other calls on us to 'find ourselves in Christ' so that the Mystery of Golgotha can be accomplished not only for *us* but also *in us*, in every individual at his or her own risk; this Paul, fearless gnostic and unstoppable tryer of reins and hearts, here comes back to life in the quality of an *epistemologist*, in a manner as yet untried by him, though it becomes him well.

One day, perhaps, there may grow on the soil of Steiner's fragmentary and scattered hints about the Pauline foundation of *The Philosophy of Freedom* a specifically anthroposophical thesis that dares to systematize this immeasurably profound parallel and translate the *gnostic* language of the Pauline letters into the *gnostic-scientific* language of the young Steiner.

Where Paul is concerned with the first and other (old and new, earthly and heavenly) human being, with the renewal of meaning and the transition to the new human being, with the six rules of gnosis, there we find in Steiner clear outlines of a theory of knowledge. The sense-perceptible world is illusion, maya, ghostly reality—not 'in itself' but through us and for us. (Paul: 'The heir, so long as he is a child, differeth nothing from a servant ... Even so we, when we were children, were in bondage under the elements of the world.' Gal., 4,1,3.) Only through pure and active thinking (that belongs to the primal beginnings of the world but can only become aware of this through human beings) will the world become fully real, when concept frees the thing from its sense-perceptible shroud and uncovers the archetypal *thought* contained within it. (Paul: 'For we know in part ... but when that which is perfect is come, then that which is in part shall be done away. When I was a child, I spake as a child, I understood as a child, I thought as a child; but when I became a man, I put away childish things. For now we see [only as though] through a glass darkly; but then face to face. Now I know in part, but then I shall know even as I am known.' I Cor., 13,9–12.)

Cognition, seen like this, proves to be the redeemer of the created world, that had become sinful in the first Adam, and also the re-creator of that world's pure and incorruptible existence in the second Adam. (Paul: 'So also is the resurrection of the dead. It is sown in corruption; it is raised in incorruption ... it is sown a natural body; it is raised a spiritual body.' I Cor., 15,42,44.) Whoever, though, has grasped the *knowledge of freedom* (Paul: 'Stand therefore, having your loins girt about with truth, and having on the breastplate of righteousness; and your feet shod with the preparation of the gospel of peace; above all, taking the shield of faith, wherewith ye shall be able to quench all the fiery darts of the wicked. And take the helmet of salvation and the sword of the spirit, which is the word of God.' Eph., 6,14–17), such a one is already in the *reality of freedom* and knows no other power over him apart from his own higher and now divine 'I'. (Steiner: 'Life of which the content is thinking is life in God.' Paul: 'Stand fast therefore in the liberty wherewith Christ hath made us free, and be not entangled again with the yoke of bondage.' Gal., 5,1.)

Having over centuries endured all the tortures of obscure or, rather, 'enlightened' imbecility, thus does the living impulse of Christianity now celebrate its triumph by means of thinking that carries thought right through into the world. Here we have another pearl, unnoticed as it lies there for all to see. Again and again, weak-minded descendants that we are, we succeed in skirting round the pearls and pecking away at our own points of view instead, especially if the pearls are not clearly labelled. What kind of Christianity can this be, we declare, if it is not even mentioned by name in this book? Surely it's time we stopped behaving like bureaucratic officials when it comes to understanding something, and begin instead to *try to reach the essence* of things. If we could pick up some imposing theological tract and, thumbing through it, realize that it's all *about* Christianity but doesn't consist of *Christianity itself!* If we could manage to stretch our understanding just this far, then we would discover the *Christianity* of *The Philosophy of Freedom* to be an outwardly invisible yet absolutely real *potential* lying hidden in this entirely philosophical *seed.*\*

Furthermore, Steiner's methodology does not permit the formulation of definitions prior to the investigation: 'The definition of an object ... can only be formulated once the scientific observation of the object has been concluded, for it contains the highest understanding of the object that it has been possible to reach.'† A few years later, when he

---

\*See R. Steiner, *Knowledge of the Higher Worlds,* op. cit. The experience with the seed recommended here offers tremendous promise particularly in this connection.
†From Steiner's commentary on Goethe. *Goethes Naturwissenschaftliche Schriften,* op. cit., Vol. 4, (Dornach, 1982, p. 202).

began to proclaim it, Christianity turned out to be the alpha and omega of every sentence he spoke or chose not to speak. This was not, however, some unexpected solution or illumination achieved through mystic grace, as many a past or present shredder of meaning would have it (and such people can now be found even among anthroposophical authors), but purely the natural *continuation* and *self-realization*, yet again, of that very same *Philosophy of Freedom*.

The most moving thing to be grasped here is: Thinking, of which the 'filioque' cannot be recognized at first, is *resurrected* thinking. It is possible to depict the history of thinking as an exact parallel of the Christian Mystery: The descent of the *Logos* was mirrored in a purely *logical* manner by the way thinking, originally unfathomable, became human. In its pre-philosophical past, the thought was identical with the world, so that it did not think the world, but thought itself as the world; consequently the world proved to be not yet the object of thinking but the thought itself. The beginning of philosophy is thus characterized by an archetypal leap from first-created unity and unthinkable undifferentiation into the state of splitting off and contrasting, in which the originally unthinkable thought gradually became aware of itself through the spontaneous pulsating of human bodies. Although it was still entirely invisible, eidetic images began to appear in it. In the twilit condition of pre-philosophical dream consciousness the dawning forces of world visibility began to break through, and now thought, hitherto *anonymous*, began to show clear signs of *synonymity* with the world. Picture, imagination, ghostly sculpture—these were the very first outlines of its awakening. In the shimmering consciousness of one like Thales they appeared as a strange panopticon of 'gods, demons, psyches'. As light created the physical eye, so did thought create the thinking eye, like a temple to which it can pay a visit from time to time. This is clearly manifest in the astonishing meaning of the word 'con-templation': The first 'thinkers' were simply *con-templars of the thought.*

The beginning of philosophy is also the beginning of the taming of thought, its coming down and gathering up in the individual human being. This can be seen in the somnambulant way the pre-Socratics functioned, for in them it is nearly always impossible to distinguish thought from myth. The pre-Socratic Logos was entirely a 'mytho-logos'; it was entirely spontaneous and supra-personal: not 'I think' but 'It thinks in me'. You find yourself up against negations when you try to come to grips with this thinking. It is not an abstraction, not a concept, not a term, not an a priori form, but rather a picture, though certainly not in the modern sense of the word, or a thing, but again not in the modern sense; a centaur, undoubtedly, in which the *picture* and the *thing* have grown together indivisibly: not a thought about the thing, but the thought of the thing itself; the thing as a thought made objective, looking for an expression of itself in the Word-Logos; and the thought as an imagination filled with 'thing-ness'. One aspect is definite: Because its mythological power was still so strong, this 'philosophy' called for a mytho-logician rather than a logician. What this means is that thought did not yet belong to human beings; it had not yet been privatized or assimilated by them. The most you can say is that it paid a visit to some 'thinker' or other (whose *whole* body it could use, as opposed to only the head). Turns of phrase, now silly, remain with us from that distant time: 'It occurred to me', or 'The idea came to me', or 'It struck me'. These are atavistic phrases now, when you consider that *modern* thinking can no longer merely 'occur' or 'appear' or 'strike' from goodness knows where, for the simple reason that its registered domicile is in the head for an unspecified period with no permit to move house.

The whole history of thinking can be traced back to this very procedure of domiciliary registration. The unfathomable and unutterable primeval thought gradually condensed until it became a *possession*: 'Thales' idea' or 'a thought belonging to Anaxagoras'. This did not happen, however, without almost seismic repercussions. (Perhaps a geologist, accustomed to exploring the cataclysms of the earth's birth pangs, will find this easier to understand than many a specialist in the history of philosophy.) These repercussions now shook the new-baked 'usurper' 'to the dividing asunder of the joints and marrow' (as Paul put it) so that even the very first stage in the appropriation of thinking was in most cases characterized by a catastrophic pulsation of *language* (thus spake Heraclitus). For this reason pre-Socratic philosophy appeared as a fire-spewing mountain: it was the final fury of cosmic thinking at being now forced irrevocably, for millennia to come, to concur with its transformation into a tedious academic nightmare. What is the history of philosophy other than the history of this extinction: the transition of thinking, alive in the cosmos, to humanized thought, right down to its 'enbrainment' (to use Max Scheler's apt expression); by which is meant its 'crucifixion', for the subsequent lot of thinking was quite literally a *Golgotha*, a *place of the skull*, in which those later 'thinkers' buried it. How painful it is to read the chapters of philosophy in which 'thinkers', having killed off thinking, hit on the idea of declaring *will* to be free and then proceed to set it free. 'And when he had said this, he went out again unto the Jews, and saith unto them, I find in him no fault at all. But ye have a custom, that I should release unto you one at the passover: will ye therefore that I release unto you the King of the Jews? Then cried they all again, saying, Not this man, but Barabbas. Now Barabbas was a robber.' (John 18, 38–40.)

Let us take the trouble to compare Plato's or Erigena's, or even Schelling's train of thought with that of Descartes or Kant. It is like stepping straight from a maternity ward into a morgue, and one, to boot, in which the dead won't lie down but put on a pretence of being alive. Perhaps this is where the true meaning of Du Bois-Reymond's *'ignoramus et ignorabimus'* belongs: We do not know and we shall not know to what extent—we are dead! This not knowing (we can now add) has never yet helped anyone come back to life.

Think of that shattering painting, by Hans Holbein the Younger, of Christ in the grave (Basle Art Gallery). Never, in my opinion, has death been portrayed like this before. (Dostoevsky once said of this picture that contemplating it threatened to rob him of his faith.) What here meets the eye is the wholesale triumph of death for which there is as yet no resurrection. Another gospel passage describes it thus: 'Lord, by this time he stinketh: for he hath been dead four days.' (John 11, 39.) Thinking today is as dead as Holbein's depiction. (Who knows, perhaps that is why its contemporary warders hold their noses and shut down their thinking capacity in their rush to recoup with death-dealing *technology* what they have neglected in cognition.) It does indeed stink, for it has been dead for (at least) four centuries.

It is not as though no attempt at all had been made at resuscitation. German idealism was perhaps the last gigantic effort—*prior* to The Philosophy of Freedom—to link human, all too human, thinking once again with cosmic thinking. But grand though it was, it failed utterly. It made the same fatal mistake as had early Christian *gnosis*: Resurrection of dead thinking was undertaken while neglecting (in typically gnostic fashion) the *material* world, the one the younger Hans Holbein painted with such shattering realism. Indeed it was no resurrection but merely a kind of magical conjuring up of the lost thinking of former days as though the blessed age of Plotinus or Proclus had returned. But Plotinus was no more. It would surely be instructive to count up how many later standard-bearers of vulgar materialism were born at the very time when Hegel in his Phenomenology of Mind or Schelling in his 'philosophy of revelation' thought they were storming the walls of heaven selflessly and without compare while in reality they were merely conjuring up the devil. No wonder the only thing actually 'resurrected' was an excess of materialistic science with its triumphant discovery of the thinking process as an internal secretion explainable only in *chemical* terms. All that yesterday's pure nobility of spirit could do was suffer magnanimously and inexpressibly at the hands of today's vulgarity of materialism.

Here the *most Christian* philosophy, *The Philosophy of Freedom*, took up the only position worthy of it: not among the heavenly ones who lent delighted ears to a *Phenomenology of Mind* or a 'philosophy of revelation', but among the earthly ones, the almost subterranean ones, who continued in cold blood to dissect corpses without discovering (according to R. Virchow's famous joke) in any one of them even the slightest trace of a soul. Here, in this mortuary, the magic words resounded: 'I SAY UNTO YOU: RISE!'

An astonishing book, according to which—let us put it in the style of Nietzsche—it is indecent, in this knowing age, *not to be a Christian!* The book that became the life of its creator and was confirmed by every pulse-beat of that life! Not in their wildest dreams had friends of all manner of magic conceived of a power as magical as that which shines in majesty through every page of this book. The heights it reaches are those from which 'all the kingdoms of the world and the glory of them' can be seen.

Here is an impossible yet heuristically justifiable question: What if the freedom that is *created* in this book (for let us never forget: no god was capable of creating what the *human being* Rudolf Steiner here created!) were not a *Christian* freedom? The answer—in a now unavoidable analogy—flashes up immediately: Then it would have been Jesus who did not go down to the Jordan, and consequently Jesus who renounced the task of fulfilling for the very first time the Mystery of the words: 'Not I, but Christ in me'.

Surely he would also have heard the voice: 'This is my beloved Son', only the voice would no longer have been that of the Father...

But here is another analogy: The image of a royal magus, led by the Christmas Star, bearing a gift to the little newborn child ... This book *The Philosophy of Freedom*—or more fundamentally *the magic of freedom*—has now become a gift such as this, laid by the freest spirit on earth before the Etheric Christ rising in the cosmos. Perhaps we shall need this clarity of sight before we (bewildered heirs to this tremendous fortune left to us by the creator of freedom) can succeed in sensing *our own* great fortune and come to understand how this book achieved the combination of such immensely reckless courage with such immense humility.

# An essential addition to all New Editions

That *The Philosophy of Freedom* remains unread and unrecognized to this day is one of the undeniable 'pathographies' of our century as it persists in clucking into the wind. Very well! But let us not forget that since the publication of this book no one has been in a position to escape the test set up by it. Whether it is read or not it catches us all out and confronts every one of us with our own *Either/Or*, the validity of which is determined not by any theoretical chit-chat but by life itself. Look at the overall *mentality* and consequent *lifestyle* of the century that has so arrogantly passed by *The Philosophy of Freedom*. Wherever the final morsels of integrity and radicality have not yet been swallowed up we arrive every time, as though bewitched, at the same diagnosis, expressible in a single word: *Absurdity*. Thus it is with the philosophers, the artists, the scientists, the spiritual mis-leaders (what else can I call them?) of the age. It is astounding to see that one of the most eminent scientific theoreticians of our time (Gaston Bachelard) finds it necessary to reduce the central question of science not to the ancient 'What is?' of Socrates and Aristotle, nor even to the 'How?' that has been acceptable until now, but to an offensive 'Why ever not?' There can be no doubt that modern science corresponds accurately to this question. And we have to ask whether this is the case with science alone...

'Why ever not?' What this means is that 'reality', unrecognized and *consequently* still unfree and inhuman, is merely left to its own devices and so begins to burst at the seams and break all records as regards 'going round the bend', so that the only path left for poor old human thinking is to become a 'statistician' capable merely of gathering *statistical* data about the things that happen: Earthquakes! Revolutions! World wars! Atom bombs! Freemasonry! Perestroika! Ozone holes!

Einstein proved: If I break one of two chairs made in the same furniture factory but now existing in two different cities, then the other one, perhaps now in Rome, will also break of its own accord at the same moment.* So what? is the rejoinder of some idle fellow whose only urge is to contribute his mite to the 'why-ever-not'-philosophy by unhesitatingly setting about eating up his own motor car.†

Let's be honest and admit that perhaps world integration (i.e. The New World Order), desired for so long and zealously aspired to, can only be smoothly achieved in one particular manner, namely if all those integrating with one another agree to put their signatures to the conclusion reached after lengthy consideration by the hero of an old Dadaist novel: *'La vie est une chose vraiment idiote.'*

I began these comments about *The Philosophy of Freedom* by mentioning those 'outsiders' who would regard me as a fantasist if I were to say that all the increasing absurdity of our age can be diagnosed on the basis of a single, unread book. Very well! The alternative is already at the door: Either Rudolf Steiner, or—Dada. Let every individual now look to the conclusions drawn by his or her own life.

---

*This is the Einstein-Podolski-Rosen Paradox. The quoted graphic example illustrating this mathematically exact version of 'Why ever not?' was formulated by Franco Selleri, Professor of Theoretical Physics at the University of Bari. Comp. F. Selleri, 'La mesure de la conscience selon von Neumann: un examen critique' in *Science et conscience. Les deux lectures de l'Univers* (Paris, 1980, p. 492f).

†See *The Guinness Book of Records*.